The Glory of God

Charlotte Rahrig

Charlotte Rahrig Ministries
Tulsa, Oklahoma

Unless otherwise indicated, all scriptural quotations are from the *King James Version* of the Bible.

The Glory of God
Published by:
Charlotte Rahrig Ministries, Inc.
P.O. Box 700565
Tulsa, OK 74170
Library of Congress Catalog Card Number: 97-92575
ISBN 0-9660646-0-7

Copyright © 1998 by Charlotte Rahrig
All rights reserved.
Reproduction of text in whole or in part without the express written consent by the author is not permitted and is unlawful according to the 1976 United States Copyright Act.

The names in the "Crisis Call" story in Chapter 4 have been changed to protect the privacy of the individuals involved.

Cover design and book production by:
DB & Associates Design & Distribution
P.O. Box 52756, Tulsa, OK 74152
Cover illustration is protected by the 1976 United States Copyright Act.
Copyright © 1998 by DB & Associates Design Group, Inc.

Editorial Consultant: Phyllis Mackall, Broken Arrow, Oklahoma

Printed in the United States of America.

Lovingly dedicated to:
My Lord and Savior
Jesus Christ

Contents

Introduction

For many years, I have read books from the back to the front. This saves me countless hours of wading through non-scriptural teaching. An author usually builds and fully develops the point he or she wants you to receive by the next to the last chapter and summarizes it in the last chapter.

Therefore, going directly to the last chapter allows me to determine if the "dish" set before me has a scriptural foundation. Finding it to be scriptural, I can then relax and enjoy the fare set before me.

I would like to save you the trouble of reading this book from the back to the front because:

1. Most people do not enjoy reading that way, and
2. I would like you to sit back, relax, and enjoy this fare set before you, fully receiving the revelation knowledge within these pages.

With that in mind, let me tell you these two things:

1. The glory of God is His Church.
2. Specifically, it is His goodness manifested through His Church.

I have seen that goodness manifested firsthand in healing, prosperity, miracles, and many other areas. This book will not only show you ways God has manifested His glory; it will show you how you may experience firsthand His glory in you.

Unto him be glory in the church by Christ Jesus throughout all ages, world without end. Amen.

Ephesians 3:21

Calling Abram out from his people, who were heathen, God was separating a chosen race to Himself. His purpose was to have them record His Word, show His nature to a pagan world, and bless the world through them by bringing the Savior of mankind from their midst.

> **...Thou art my servant, O Israel, in whom I wilt be glorified.**
>
> **Isaiah 49:3**

God is not a respecter of persons, and He wants us to partake of that same promise! Paul writes in Ephesians 3:

> **That the Gentiles should be fellow-heirs, and of the same body and partakers of his promise in Christ by the gospel.**
>
> **Ephesians 3:6**

The reason why God manifests His glory in a people is to draw us to Himself. God desires to show His glory in the Church for these two reasons:

1. To show that He is God, and there is no other.
2. To draw us to Him so we may partake of that glory. Jesus spoke of this glory in John 17:

> **And the glory which thou gavest me I have given them; that they may be one, even as we are one.**
>
> **John 17:22**

So relax, pull up a chair, and come and dine. We are about to partake of God's Word, see His glory, and experience that glory in us.

> **To whom God would make known what is the riches of the glory of this mystery among the Gentiles; which is Christ in you, the hope of glory.**
>
> **Colossians 1:27**

— *Charlotte Rahrig*
Tulsa, Oklahoma

Part 1

The Glory of God Manifested Through Healing

Chapter 1
Grandma's Story

Laura Lela was her real name, but her whole family called her Pansy. The locket I wear, now more than 90 years old, bears the script initials "PH," representing her maiden name, Pansy Harrison.

I remember how proud my family was when they discovered that President William Henry Harrison was a distant relative. After further searching of the family tree revealed another relative who had been hanged as a horse thief, they decided to stop researching.

Grandpa gave Grandma the locket on her sixteenth birthday. They married the next year and then spent more than 60 years together. Their first baby, Thelma, put teething marks on that locket.

Grandma was a beautiful young woman who went about the house singing while she did her chores. She was joyful and happy, and Grandpa said she brightened any room she entered. Then tragedy struck.

Grandpa took Thelma, who was then almost 3, to a circus. There were no food inspectors in those days, and Grandpa unknowingly bought Thelma some tainted popcorn. Consequently, Thelma developed dysentery and became very ill.

Her parents took her to a doctor who turned out to be a quack. He gave them wrong advice, telling them not to give her a drop of anything to eat, or it would kill her. Faithfully following his advice, they watched Thelma grow sicker each day.

Realizing that something was seriously wrong, they took her to the next town in search of another doctor. After the second doctor examined Thelma, he began to yell at her parents, telling them they were killing their baby. It was too late. His efforts to save the baby failed. Thelma died.

Wordless Grief

Grandma never said a word when her baby died, nor did she shed a tear. Fifty years passed. Grandma went from being a very joyful woman to being a very bitter woman. She bore two sons and another daughter, Marzelle, who was my mother. Yet in all those years, she never shed a tear for her firstborn child.

Crippling rheumatoid arthritis took a heavy toll in her life. She went from walking normally and easily to struggling to walk with a cane and then a walker. Finally, she ended up in a wheelchair.

Grandma seemed to like only a few of her nine grandchildren, and she wasn't exactly fond of other people. I can remember a day my mom took my sister and me to visit her. Grandma stood at the door, hollering and waving her cane, "Marzelle, you can come in, and Cookie (that's me) can come in, but that little — (my small sister) can't come in!"

On another visit to her when I was about 12 years old, Grandma tried to tear the hair out of my little brother's head. He was about 2 years old, and he had been crying for my mother when I was preparing to babysit him.

A Hopeless Situation

Poor Grandpa did everything he could to get Grandma help. He took her to many doctors and tried many remedies. Once he even took her to have gold shot into her veins. Nothing worked. There seemed to be no relief for her continual, non-stop pain and misery. And the pain increased as her condition worsened.

Her knuckles enlarged, and her fingers began to twist like pretzels. If she pointed her hands forward, her fingers pointed to the sides. Eventually, her arms became locked against her sides. She was unable to lift them, so a terrible chafing started and reached the point of bleeding when we tried to insert a wash cloth between her arms and body at bath time.

She weighed more than 200 pounds, so we had to purchase a hydraulic lift to get Grandma in and out of bed. Another was attached to the top of the car to get her in and out of it for doctors' appointments.

One day as her sister was pushing her wheelchair, it hit a stone, and out fell Grandma! Both of her legs broke in two places, and her hip also broke. Now she was in a full body cast that extended from under her arms to her feet.

All Hope Is Gone

Grandma had always hoped to walk again someday, but all her hopes were dashed forever when the doctor explained that because of her advanced age (late 70s), her bones would never knit together properly; and even without the arthritis, she would never walk. We moved in with our grandparents, and Mom became Grandma's 24-hour-a-day caregiver.

A cow bell was hung in the hall. Attached to it was a taunt fishing line tied to one of Grandma's fingers. If she couldn't bear the pain anymore during the night, she could pull on the line, and the noise of the bell would summon Mom.

Possibly Grandma would want her foot moved one inch in a different direction. Mom would gently cradle her foot between her hands and attempt, ever so gently, to move the foot an inch. Grandma would scream in pain! The next morning, worried neighbors would come over because they had heard her screams in the night.

I want you to get a picture of this woman. She was very large, her arms were locked to her sides, and she had been an invalid for $4^1/2$ long years. The slightest amount of pressure on her skin caused discoloration. Black and blue marks covered her body from our simply bathing her. As we bathed her, odors were pungent from under her arms and other areas where it was difficult to touch her without pain. Tubes of different creams surrounded her bed. They were used in an attempt to prevent bedsores. Grandma suffered terribly.

Good News!

One day, Grandpa burst through the front door talking rapidly and with great excitement. He had heard some wonderful news! He said a man was going around the country preaching in a tent, healing people. Even people who were in wheelchairs were being healed!

We could hardly believe our ears! Grandpa insisted that many of these healings had been verified by doctors. We lived in southern Florida, and this man was coming to Pensacola, in northern Florida. We had hope!

We had been raised in a traditional denomination that did not believe that God still heals — or that healing came from God. We were totally ignorant of the Word.

As painful as it was for Grandma, we packed her into a little white Corvair that had been their 50th anniversary present, and we headed for Pensacola. Desperate for help, we would have gone anywhere.

A Touch of Faith

We found hundreds and hundreds of people lined up for healing in the tent. Row after row, Oral Roberts walked down the lines, first touching one head, "In the Name of Jesus," then crossing his arm over that one to touch the next person, "In the Name of Jesus!" Person after person, row after row, a touch of faith, and then on to the next.

Although I was only 14, I was rather strong, so I was in charge of Grandma's wheelchair. I had to struggle with it, because the wheels sank into the sawdust. We stood in the healing line for a long time. Without a break in his rhythm, like a heartbeat, the evangelist continued down each row, touching one, then another.

Now he was at the front of our row! I leaned out to watch. Here and there we could hear happy screams from people who had been healed. My heart was beating so fast. "Please heal my grandma...please heal my grandma..." My thoughts raced at the impossibility of it, "...but please!"

Now he was just a few people in front of us. Hand over hand: "In the Name of Jesus! In the Name of Jesus!" He started to put his hand on Grandma's head, then suddenly stopped in midair, not touching her at all!

A Look of Love

Strangely, he put both hands on his hips and began to stare down at her with a big grin. At least a full minute passed. He continued to stand there staring with this big grin. No words could describe the look on his face. There was so much love in that grin. It was like a father looking at a child he loves.

I continued to clutch the handles of the wheelchair, my knuckles almost white — expecting. Grandma, in the meantime, had been sitting there staring into the sawdust, embarrassed to look up. Oral Roberts continued his stare, grinning all the time. Soon, Grandma sheepishly looked up, and their eyes met.

Out of the corner of her eye came a little tear. It began to trace a path down her cheek. Oral Roberts went on without ever touching Grandma — physically touching, that is. That tear was like a plug broken in this woman who sat there enslaved to bitterness. It was followed by another tear, then more tears, then a flood. She began bawling and wailing.

Remember, this is a woman who had not cried in the last 50 years! I was so upset. The man of God had gone by without touching my grandma, and we had come all this way.

A Torrent of Tears

We assumed Grandma was crying because she hadn't been prayed for. She cried the whole trip back home, throughout the night, and throughout the next day. She cried when awake and asleep. Almost two weeks went by, and she continued to cry, never telling us what was wrong.

We all felt so bad for her! Passing each other in the living room, we would just shrug our shoulders in helplessness as we heard the pitiful cries coming from her bedroom. Then, after two weeks, the crying stopped. Grandma began to talk.

She talked about Thelma. This had been a taboo subject previously. She talked about all the guilt she had experienced during the years since Thelma's death. Tears streamed as she told of the times Thelma would drag her little red chair over to her while she was doing the laundry with a scrub board in an old-fashioned washtub.

"Read, Mommy, read," Thelma would plead as she clutched a little picture book, but Grandma had been too busy to read. She shared how much she had loved the little girl she felt she had killed. Fifty years' worth of emotions poured out.

I remember hugging her, comforting her, and assuring her she had done everything she knew to do at the time, and one day she would be reunited with Thelma.

A New Creature

When Grandma finally got it all cried and talked out, she stated reading her Bible and praying. Talking to God, she became transformed! No one who knew her could believe she was the same person. With a newfound warmth and friendliness, she started developing loving relationships with all her grandchildren. Grandma had changed! But she was still confined to her wheelchair.

Almost a year and a half passed since Pensacola. Then news came that Oral Roberts was coming with his tent to the polo grounds in West Palm Beach. This was just a few blocks from our house, and we were all very excited!

I had learned from the Pensacola experience that Oral Roberts would stay in a travel trailer in the back of the tent until all the preliminaries of the meeting were complete. Then, after the worship service and the offering, he would walk onto the platform just as he was being introduced, and he would immediately begin to preach.

When we arrived at the West Palm Beach crusade, I asked Mom and my brother to take Grandma into the back of the tent and wait for me. Then I ran to the back of the tent outside a travel trailer I was certain must contain Oral Roberts. The weeds were tall, and there was only moonlight, but I leaned against the trailer beside its steps and began my vigil.

After about 45 minutes, the door flew open and out came a tall, powerful-looking man. In the moonlight, he seemed to be much larger than in Pensacola. He saw me at once and asked what I needed.

A Plea for Help

Half-shaking, I explained how we had brought my grandma to Pensacola, and he wouldn't pray for her, but she was here tonight, and would he pray for her?

"Yes," he said, "I'll pray for your grandmother." He asked me who she was and where she would be in the tent. I explained she would be the white-haired woman in a wheelchair in the back. Oral Roberts started toward his usual entrance near the stage up front, and I ran excitedly to the back of the tent. But as I entered, my heart sank. It looked like a sea of wheelchairs, and elderly ladies were in half of them. "Oh no!" I thought. "He's not going to know who she is. He won't know who to pray for!"

I ran to Grandma's chair, grabbed its handles, and began to drag it backwards through the sawdust. She was so heavy, the wheels sank in the sawdust, but I managed to drag the chair into the aisle, which provided us a clear view of the platform.

Oral Roberts had just been introduced and was leaning over the pulpit to the microphone, preparing to say something. I had Grandma in the aisle, jumping up and down, trying to catch his attention, all the time pointing to Grandma with an arm stretched up in the air. "This is her," I was screaming in my mind. "This is her! Do you see her? I'm the one you just talked to outside. This is my grandma!"

Then, before Oral Roberts had a chance to speak a word, this woman, my grandmother, who had suffered so many years, whose arms were locked at her sides, who had been an invalid for six years, whose legs and hip had been broken, whose hands were gnarled and twisted, shot her arms straight up in the air!

I Saw Crooked Bones Straighten!

I was holding the handles of Grandma's wheelchair. This put her hands directly in front of my face. Then, right before my eyes, her crooked bones were totally straightened! Grandma bolted to her feet and took off running up that center aisle, screaming at the top of her voice, "I'm healed! I'm healed!"

I stared in unbelief. My first thought was, "She's been faking all these years!" Then, regaining my senses, I realized, "I've just witnessed crooked bones become straight. I've seen Grandma's agony and pain. She's been healed — and it's too good to believe!"

Grandma came running back toward me, grabbed me by my blouse, threw me into her wheelchair, and began to drag me around in the sawdust, screaming, "I'm healed! I'm healed!"

That night we all sat in awe and watched in disbelief as Grandma prepared tea and served it to us. It was as if we had seen a ghost.

The hydraulic lift on the car was sold, the one in the house was sold, and the ramp over the stairs was removed, along with anything else that indicated an invalid had ever lived there. Grandma lived several more years after that, dying in her 80s, still healed.

I was 16 years old the night Grandma was healed. At age 16, I had come face-to-face with the manifested glory of God.

Questions To Ask Yourself About Grandma's Story

1. Why do you think Grandma did not cry when her baby died?

Looking diligently lest any man fail of the grace of God; lest any root of bitterness springing up trouble you, and thereby many be defiled.

Hebrews 12:15

2. Do you think God only sees the tears shed from physical eyes?

Thou tellest my wanderings: put thou my tears into thy bottle: are they not in thy book?

Psalm 56:8

I cried with my whole heart; hear me, O Lord: I will keep thy statutes.

Psalm 119:145

3. Why do you think Grandma did not receive a physical manifestation of healing the first time she was in a prayer line?

And when ye stand praying, forgive, if any have aught against any: that your father also which is in heaven may forgive you of your trespasses.

But if ye do not forgive, neither will your Father which is in heaven forgive your trespasses.

Mark 11:25,26

4. Although the story does not specifically state that Grandma had forgiven God, how did her behavior reflect this?

...for out of the abundance of the heart the mouth speaketh.

Matthew 12:34

I will greatly rejoice in the Lord, my soul shall be joyful in my God; for he hath clothed me with the garments of salvation, he hath covered me with the robe of righteousness, as a bridegroom decketh himself with ornaments, and as a bride adorneth herself with her jewels.

For as the earth bringeth forth her bud, and as the garden causeth the things that are sown in it to spring forth; so the Lord God will cause righteousness and praise to spring forth before all the nations.

Isaiah 61:10,11

5. Why do you think Grandma received spiritual healing for her soul in the first prayer line and physical healing for her body in the second tent meeting without having hands actually laid on her?

And he said unto him, Arise, go thy way: thy faith hath made thee whole.

Luke 17:19

To another the working of miracles; to another prophecy; to another discerning of spirits; to another divers kinds of tongues; to another the interpretation of tongues:

But all these worketh that one and the selfsame Spirit, dividing to every man severally as he will.

1 Corinthians 12:10,11

Has God Healed Us Or Not?

Unforgiveness blocks healing. How often have I heard that? How many times, new to the Word, had I pictured God on His throne withholding healing, saying, "When you do all the 'ifs' to obtain my promises, I will let go of this healing and bless you."

Grandma's story was a perfect example of this. Grandma could not have received her healing with unforgiveness in her heart. She shared with me that she had been bitter against God, but she not not realized that fact.

This made sense to me. Grandma could not expect to receive healing from the One against whom she was bitter. However, as I grew to know God better and understand His nature better, I knew there had to be an explanation to bridge the gap between unforgiveness blocking healing and the fact that we were healed 2000 years ago on the cross of Calvary.

Imagine how you would feel if news had just been delivered to you that your child was missing in dangerous woods. Everything in your life would come to an immediate halt. You would have no rest until that child was found. Your thoughts would be filled with plans for rescue. Your heart would be aching with love for that child.

The Word tells us we are created in God's image. Our earthly love for our children is just a small taste of God's love for us. If love were an ocean, we could hold only a teacupful. God's love is the whole ocean.

As a footnote to this thought, if you knock the bottom out of the teacup, you can pour the whole ocean through it. The bottom represents "self." Laying aside "I," "me," and "my" allows God's love to be poured out through you to a lost and dying world.

Returning to our question: If healing was already an accomplished fact 2000 years ago, how can unforgiveness block healing? Isn't God actually saying that you receive by works instead of by faith? Is He not withholding blessing until you tap dance to His tune? No!

The Way to Healing

The best way I can describe the answer is to give you the example of a road map. You are at a certain city on the map called Needs Healing. God has built a superhighway from Point A, where you are, to Point B, which is a city called You Have It. The superhighway is called The Way.

It is easy to go directly to the city called You Have It. The way has been provided. It is a superhighway, so it has no stoplights. What it does have, however, are many exits and rest stops. This is because we have a free will that allows us to leave the highway whenever we choose.

Some people get on that superhighway and zoom straight from Point A to Point B. They do not look to the left or the right. They do not question the integrity of the mapmaker. They saw on the map the direction to go, they believed the map, and they acted on what they believed.

Others start the journey on the exact same road. They are excited about the trip, but they begin to look at the signs around them. One exit is called Ignorance. It leads to a small city where people do not understand what the cross provided for them. They have heard of covenant, but it is just another word to them.

The preachers in their pulpits preach that the time of miracles is over and healing is not for today. They have even put up some billboards along the road as you approach their exit. The billboards proclaim, "Sickness is God's way to teach you something." They show a man in a wheelchair reading his Bible with a noble look on his face. Another billboard shows a nurse witnessing to a teenager in a hospital bed. This sign proclaims, "Sometimes God has to put us where He can get our attention." So many people have exited at this first exit, they never have to bother with the ones to come.

The next exit is called Unforgiveness. It is a little city tucked neatly away in the woods. Sometimes you do not even notice it is there. Often you may not even know that you have come to visit this city until you try to leave. It is a very difficult city to get out of on your own.

The billboards approaching this exit show everything from incest to divorce. They proclaim, "Come, be comforted in Unforgiveness." "We want to hear how you have been treated." "Rehearse your hurts here." Many have strayed off The Way to healing by this exist.

There are many other exits that try to tempt you off The Way. I will not try to list them all. There is only one last exit that must be mentioned. This exit is for the city called Out of Love.

People will be zooming down The Way and suddenly find themselves visiting this city. Often, they will have to stop their cars and try to think back to the point where they missed it and turned to this destintion. They did not intend to turn. They just found themselves here. The billboards say things like, "You have the right to be mad" while picturing abortion clinics and drunk drivers.

Others drive many miles from Point A. They are just about to arrive at Point B. They have resisted all the exits and kept their eyes on the road. They have been diligent and unwavering, but they begin to feel weary. They are tired of driving. Behold! What have we here? A rest stop.

Not knowing they are just moments from their destination, they say, "I'm not getting anywhere. If I was like other people, I would be there already." They pull their car aside, close their eyes, and go to sleep. They never make it to their destination.

My question is, "Was the way provided?" Yes! God has already provided healing for us. He has paved the way and given us the map. We are the ones who detour from the way. His desire is for us to receive what He has provided.

Grandma Takes All Three Exits

Grandma took all three exits! The first had been Unforgiveness. In that town, they serve daily drinks of bitterness and despair, and the drinks are on the house. Broken spirits are common here, and a broken spirit dries up the bones, according to Proverbs 17:22. Few people are able to linger long in this town without serious illnesses overtaking them.

The next exit Grandma took had been Ignorance. She had no idea what the Bible said about healing until she began to read it. Had she known what was provided in the covenant, she would have had the faith to reach out and take her healing earlier.

Her third exit had been Out of Love. She had to get out of that town before she could get back on The Way. I remember how shocked the neighbors had been at her changed attitude. They couldn't believe she was the same woman! After reading her Bible and being healed of unforgiveness, she had changed. She had become sweet and gentle.

I knew Grandma was healed of unforgiveness when the man of God stood staring at her. She related to me that it had felt like she was looking into the eyes of God. She experienced conviction and true repentance for blaming God for the death of her child. The days of crying represented her repenting and a cleansing.

The Master's Look

As I was writing this book, I thought, "All right, Lord, I was there. I saw repentance come from a simple look." I felt that in the same way God pours out His anointing by the laying on of hands through His servants, He had looked at Grandma through His servant Oral Roberts.

"But God, I have to have Scripture," I prayed. "Can You show me one place in the New Testament where a look caused repentance?" God immediately reminded me of Peter's denial.

> **And Peter said, Man, I know not what thou sayest. And immediately, while he yet spake, the cock crew.**
>
> **And the Lord turned, and looked upon Peter. And Peter remembered the word of the Lord, how he had said unto him, Before the cock crow, thou shalt deny me thrice.**
>
> **And Peter went out, and wept bitterly.**
>
> **Luke 22:60-62**

According to *Strong's Concordance,* the word "look" as it is used in this scripture means "to look on, to observe fixedly, to discern clearly." In other words, all things are laid open and bare before the stare of God. And I have always heard that what the Holy Spirit reveals, He heals. Thank You, Jesus.

The Good Shepherd

There have been multitudes of wonderful Word of Faith books written on the subject of healing. Because of that, I will not try to teach you on our covenant and the basics of healing.

This book is about the glory of God. I am attempting to answer any possible doubts you may still have that are preventing your tapping into that glory.

At the end of this chapter are listed some excellent books and authors along with Scripture references. If you have not read them, read them. God wants you healed! Sickness does not glorify God. As stated earlier, the glory of God is His goodness manifested through His Church.

Do you still have lingering doubts that God *always* wants the Church to be healed? Think about the following illustration I heard from one preacher.

John 10:10 tells us that Jesus is the Good Shepherd. Let's suppose you lived in Bible times. You have heard all your life about the Good Shepherd.

One day the people begin shouting that the Good Shepherd is coming. They begin to line the streets, cheering. Your heart is beating with anticipation as you observe the scene. The Good Shepherd is coming! You are finally going to get to see the man you have heard so much about.

Soon you catch a glimpse of him coming in the distance. First you see his staff. It is covered with jewels. Next, as he draws closer, you notice how beautifully he is clothed. Oh yes, this is surely the Good Shepherd. He is everything you were told to expect. He is so regal and noble looking.

Then he moves closer, and his flock comes into view. They are all so emaciated, their ribs are sticking out. They have untreated wounds caused by the bites of wolves who have tried to kill and eat them. They are bleeding and hungry. One is limping because a broken leg had gone untreated and not mended properly. What thoughts are running through your mind? You would be thinking that this was not a good shepherd. It does not matter what people had told you about him. He is a terrible shepherd. All you have to do is look at his sheep to tell that. The shepherd, you see, is judged by the condition of his flock!

Jesus is the Good Shepherd (John 10:11), not the bad shepherd. We are His flock. The flock is the glory of the shepherd. A happy, well-fed, healed flock reflects the tender care of a good shepherd. We are under His tender care and are a direct reflection of Him. His goodness toward us by healing our bodies is one way He manifests His glory in the Church!

Healing Books

And Jesus Healed Them All, Gloria Copeland
Bodily Healing and the Atonement, Kenneth E. Hagin
Christ the Healer, F. F. Bosworth
God's Creative Power for Healing, Charles Capps
God's Medicine, Kenneth E. Hagin
God's Will for Healing, Gloria Copeland
Healing Belongs to Us, Kenneth E. Hagin
Healing Scriptures, Kenneth E. Hagin
Hear and Be Healed, Kenneth E. Hagin
Is Healing for All?, Frederick Price
Seven Hindrances To Receiving Healing, Kenneth Hagin Jr.
You Are Healed, Kenneth Copeland

Healing Scriptures

Genesis 20:17
Exodus 15:26
Leviticus 26:3-5
Deuteronomy 4:40
Deuteronomy 28:1-3
Deuteronomy 30:9,16,20
Psalm 6:2
Psalm 71:16
Psalm 73:26
Psalm 91:10-16
Proverbs 9:11
Isaiah 43:1,2
Isaiah 53:4,5
Isaiah 65:22
Matthew 4:23,24
Matthew 19:2
Mark 16:15-18

Luke 22:50,51
John 5:2-14
Acts 3:1-10
Acts 4:10
Acts 4:29,30
Romans 4:17,19-21
Romans 8:11-13
1 Corinthians 12:28-30
Ephesians 6:1-3
1 Thessalonians 5:23
2 Timothy 1:7
Hebrews 2:14,15
Hebrews 4:14-16
Hebrews 12:12,13
James 5:14-16
1 Peter 2:24
1 John 3:8
3 John 2

Chapter 2
God's Dentistry

Three of my five children had similar teeth. Each had a gaping hole between their two front teeth large enough to pass the end of your little finger through. My 10-year-old, Gil, and my 8-year-old, Sally, both had spread-out "buck teeth." Jacob, who was 6, had an extreme "buck." Each child experienced different reactions to this unsightly condition.

Gil was always complaining. Sally did not have much to say about the matter, and Jacob was satisfied with his teeth just the way they were.

After listening to Gil complain for some time, I made an appointment with an orthodontist. All the preliminary information was taken, along with an impression of his teeth. The dentist then proceeded to explain what would happen to Gil. Pointing to the gum area between the two front teeth, he explained that he would do some minor surgery in that area.

It seems there was a piece of cartilage-like substance there that would first have to be removed, because if it was not removed, the braces would not be able to pull the teeth together. The dentist assured Gil that the procedure would be painless, because he would numb the area. I left the office satisfied that my son would soon be on his way to a happy smile.

No sooner had we left the office than Gil began to cry. It seems the only word he had heard was "surgery," and he did not want any part of it! The more he talked about it, the more fearful he became. After arriving home, he gathered support on his side, convincing his father that we probably could not afford braces just then. Now the two of them fussed all day. Eventually, it did not seem worth the battle.

I was trying to fry chicken, and there was Gil behind me, whining about not getting braces. Simply frustrated, I put down my cooking utensils, turned around, and said, "Okay, so don't get braces!" Then, laying my hand across his mouth, I prayed, "Father, in Jesus' Name, I ask You to straighten these teeth." Gil turned, running away thrilled that he had finally worn me down. I went back to the pressing matter of the moment, cooking dinner.

Three months passed, and the subject of braces had not been mentioned again. We were on our way to church on a Sunday morning. In typical fashion, the kids were bouncing all around the back seat. Gil had unhooked his seat belt and was leaning his head over the front seat. I spun around to tell him to get back into his seat immediately, but to my surprise, I found myself staring at a perfect set of teeth!

The hole, along with the "fan" arrangement and the "buck," were gone. His set of teeth were now candidates for a toothpaste ad. They were so straight and tight together, we later found it difficult to floss between them.

I screamed, "Your teeth are straight! Your teeth are straight!" Gil stared at me in disbelief. He quickly leaned all the way forward to the rear view mirror to look for himself. Flopping back in his seat, he sat in stunned silence. I was now the one bouncing around in my seat, rejoicing at the goodness of God and the power of the Name of Jesus.

Then I noticed Sally. There she sat, arms crossed across her chest, with a scowl on her face and her bottom lip sticking out.

"What's wrong with you, Sally? Aren't you happy for your brother? His teeth are straight!" Sally never looked in my direction. She kept her eyes fixed straight ahead with an unbroken resolve to show her anger.

As her arms tightened across her chest, she blurted out in dismay, "Why didn't God straighten my teeth?" I explained to her that we had prayed for Gil's teeth to be straightened three months earlier and that God would do the same for her. Still she would not look up. Remaining in the same pouting position, she declared she did not want to wait three months. I told her she did not have to, because if we believe when we pray, the Word of God says we can have the things we desire.

This was language Sally understood. We were members of Gospel Bill's video club.[1] Each month, Willie George Ministries in Tulsa sent us a tape, and each month, Sally watched the tape 30 to 40 times until the following month, when the next tape would arrive. She had the Word sown in her heart big time!

Sally's frown turned into an expression of hope. "God will straighten my teeth now?" she asked.

"Yes, Sally, He will. All you have to do is believe."

Sally sighed with relief. It was like she was thinking, "Oh, is that all I have to do? I thought I was going to have to do something hard." She asked me to pray. Closing her eyes, she leaned her face forward so I could lay hands on her mouth.

I prayed, "Father, in Jesus' Name, I ask You to straighten these teeth, and Sally would like it done now. She does not want to wait. We thank You for the answer."

Sally leaned back, satisfied that she would get her desire. No more than five minutes later, she started screaming and shrieking, "My teeth are moving! My teeth are moving!" She was holding her mouth with her hands.

There have been times in my life that I have been excited and filled with joy. Probably the birth of each of my children and the arrival of my adopted child were the highlights of my joy on Earth as a human. But that joy could not compare to the feeling of being in the manifested presence of the glory of God!

The Father of the universe was manifesting His presence in our car by straightening my child's teeth. He is the God who had scooped out the valleys, formed the hills, and flung the stars into space. He had parted the Red Sea, shut lions' mouths, and made the sun stand still. This was God, and He was in my car! He was moving on my child's behalf! All my surroundings seemed to fade into oblivion. I was engulfed in a bubble of light and joy.

"Jacob," I yelled, "let me pray for your teeth!" Jacob quickly cupped his hands over his mouth, turned in his seat, and hid his face in the corner of the door. "But I want to be a beaver and build a dam," he wailed.

Pleading with Jacob, I asked him again to *please* let me pray for his teeth. He finally agreed I could pray "just a little." He said he wanted his teeth to go halfway in and halfway together. Jacob did not want his beaver building plans ruined.

I laid hands on Jacob's mouth, praying exactly as he had requested: "Lord, Jacob only wants his teeth to go halfway in and halfway together, in Jesus' Name."

By morning, Sally had her new set of teeth. They had moved into perfect alignment. They no longer fanned out. They no longer were "buck teeth." She no longer had a space between her two front teeth. Instead, she had a beautiful smile!

Within one week, Jacob's teeth had moved exactly halfway in and halfway together, precisely as he had requested. God had shown Himself strong on behalf of my children. He had manifested His glory in them for the world to see.

Questions To Ask Yourself About God's Dentistry

1. Why do you think God allows children to be born with physical defects?

> **Thou madest him [man] to have dominion over the works of thy hands; thou hast put all things under his feet.**
>
> **Psalm 8:6**

Verily I say unto you, Whatsoever ye shall bind on earth shall be bound in heaven: and whatsoever ye shall loose on earth shall be loosed in heaven.

Matthew 18:18

2. Why did Gil become more afraid as he spoke about the surgery?

For verily I say unto you, That whosoever shall say unto this mountain, Be thou removed, and be thou cast into the sea; and shall not doubt in his heart, but shall believe that those things which he saith shall come to pass; he shall have whatsoever he saith.

Mark 11:23

Death and life are in the power of the tongue: and they that love it shall eat the fruit thereof.

Proverbs 18:21

3. Gil seemed to be appeasing his mother, allowing her to pray so he would not have to have surgery. Why do you think the prayer was answered?

If ye shall ask any thing in my name, I will do it.

John 14:14

And in that day ye shall ask me nothing. Verily, verily, I say unto you, Whatsoever ye shall ask the Father in my name, he will give it you.

John 16:23

4. Why was Sally able to receive an instant manifestation of healing?

But Jesus turned him about, and when he saw her, he said, Daughter, be of good comfort; thy faith hath made thee whole....

Matthew 9:22

Then Jesus answered and said unto her, O woman, great is thy faith: be it unto thee even as thou wilt. And her daughter was made whole from that very hour.

Matthew 15:28

5. Why did Jacob's teeth only straighten halfway?

Therefore I say unto you, What things soever ye desire, when ye pray, believe that ye receive them, and ye shall have them.

Mark 11:24

Sowing for Glory

Of the three distinct miracles God performed in straightening the children's teeth, Sally's miracle was the most notable. She received the instant manifestation so many people desire.

Many of us yearn to walk in the miraculous. We turn on the television and witness a crusade healing. A wheelchair is rolled off the stage empty, or crutches are thrown away. Another program features a guest who tells what wonderful things God has done in his life.

Our heart cries out, "Why not *me*, God? Why not *my* children?" The guest on the television program tells you what he did to bring about the miracle in his life, and you do exactly what he did — and nothing happens.

Personal Gospel

The reason nothing happens when you do the same thing others do is because this is a personal Gospel; it is not a set of magic formulas. This Gospel must be real to you personally. God is a personal God who desires a personal relationship with His children.

Loving you enough to give His only Son on your behalf, He reaches down to lift you just as high as your faith yields to Him.

The healing books listed in the previous chapter will tell you of many instances where the Word records healings that happened as a result of people's faith. A few examples are:

Matthew 9:22,29; 15:28

Mark 2:5; 5:34; 10:52

Luke 5:20; 8:48; 17:19

Acts 3:16; 14:9

There are no limits to what God will do for you — except your faith.

King Asa's Truth

We find in Second Chronicles 14-16 an interesting story concerning Asa, king of Judah. When surrounded by his enemies, he prayed, "...O Lord, thou art our God; let not man prevail against thee" (2 Chronicles 14:11).

Asa had tapped into a great truth here. This truth is that if anyone or anything tries to come against God's people, they are coming against God Himself!

Jesus taught this truth in Luke 9:48:

> **...Whosoever shall receive this child in my name receiveth me: and whosoever shall receive me receiveth him that sent me....**

It is easy to read this Scripture and picture that if we accept or reject a sweet little curly-haired child, we are accepting or rejecting Jesus. Little children are so innocent; so deserving to be loved. That's just how it should be, but we must understand that we are also God's children.

You may be sitting reading this book with a 5 o'clock shadow across your face. You may have a pot belly and a king-sized pack of cigarettes in your shirt pocket. If you have asked Jesus to come into your heart and forgive you of your sins, you are God's child. Salvation is based on what Jesus did for us, not on what we do for Him.

> **And be found in him, not having mine own righteousness, which is of the law, but that which is through the faith of Christ, the righteousness which is of God by faith.**
>
> **Philippians 3:9**

Characteristics of Baby Christians

The Book of Hebrews speaks of the difference between baby Christians who need milk and mature Christians who can take strong meat. Do you know what makes the difference? It is not what you might think. It is not if you cuss, smoke, or go to church. Babes are those who are unskilled in the word of righteousness.

> **For when for the time ye ought to be teachers, ye have need that one teach you again which be the first principles of the oracles of God; and are become such as have need of milk, and not of strong meat,**
>
> **For every one that useth milk is unskillful in the word of righteousness: for he is a babe.**
>
> **But strong meat belongeth to them that are of full age, even those who by reason of use have their senses exercised to discern both good and evil.**
>
> **Hebrews 5:12-14**

The Holy Spirit's Work

The Holy Spirit convicts of sin. He ever so gently prods you to deal with certain things in your life that need to be eliminated. As you read the Word, He is washing you, according to Ephesians 5:26.

The light of the Word reveals one area at a time. The Holy Spirit then helps you overcome in each of those areas. He is always upholding you and drawing you closer to the Father.

Satan, on the other hand, is the accuser of the brethren, according to Revelation 12:10. I have found he constantly reminds you of your sins all at once, trying to overwhelm you with your own lack of ability to deal with certain problems.

Condemnation is the result of his activities. However, no repentance comes as a result of condemnation. It is the goodness of God that leads us to repentance, Romans 2:4 says. When we feel condemned, we mistakingly run from God instead of to Him.

Mysteries of Grace

The apostle Paul in Ephesians begins to unfold to the Church mysteries of the grace of God. It is a marvelous epistle of freedom and revelation of promises to those who partake of the Gospel in Christ.

This epistle also introduces us to the unseen realm of principalities and powers. Personally, Ephesians is one of my favorite books in the New Testament. But sometimes when I read it, I have to read the same verse several times before I grasp its full meaning. I would summarize all of Ephesians this way:

God rules.

You rule with Him in Christ Jesus.

The devil does not like it.

You have power over the devil.

Do not listen to his lies.

Take what is yours.

Rule!

Let's say you go forward in a prayer line to have hands laid on you for healing. In the unseen realm, you are a believer walking boldly to the throne to partake of your covenant promises. Again, we cannot cover all information about the covenant here. Read all that is available from the previous book list.

When you seek healing, Satan will immediately begin to attack your mind, reminding you of every fault you have. His purpose is to condemn you so you will have doubts that God will heal you. "You are so unworthy," he will tell you. "You are not good enough for God to heal you." Allowing doubt to enter, you fail to reach out and grab hold of what is rightfully yours!

Asa Is Corrected

Let's return to the story of King Asa. He depended on God for victory. In Second Chronicles 16, this same king is found making a league with the king of Syria to handle his problems instead of turning to God.

He is corrected by Hanani, who reminded him that when he had relied on the Lord, his enemies had been delivered into his hands. Then we find Hanani saying something very important about God. It helps us understand His nature and shows us how He feels about His children. Hanani said in Second Chronicles 16:9:

> **For the eyes of the Lord run to and fro throughout the whole earth, to shew himself strong in the behalf of them whose heart is perfect toward him....**

Strong's Concordance notes that the word "perfect" means "complete" or "just." (See Strong's numbers 5046, 2677, 2675, and 5048 for more detailed information.) That is us. We are complete in Him!

> **And ye are complete in him, which is the head of all principality and power....**
>
> **Colossians 2:10**

We are the "just." Jesus has justified us through the shedding of His blood.

> **Knowing that a man is not justified by the works of the law, but by the faith of Jesus Christ, even we have believed in Jesus Christ, that we might be justified by the faith of Christ, and not by the works of the law: for by the works of the law shall no flesh be justified.**
>
> **Galatians 2:16**

Hebrews tells us further:

> **But ye are come unto mount Sion, and unto the city of the living God, the heavenly Jerusalem, and to an innumerable company of angels,**
>
> **To the general assembly and church of the firstborn, which are written in heaven, and to God the Judge of all, and the spirits of just men made perfect.**
>
> **Hebrews 12:22,23**

Complete and Just

So we see that we are both complete and just. Our hearts have been made perfect in Him! That means His eyes are running to and fro looking to show Himself strong on our behalf. We can rely on God. He is on our side.

When sickness, disease, or any other foe comes against us, they have come against God! This is the confidence that allows us to boldly reach out and take the promises.

King Asa had wandered so far away from relying on God that eventually he "sought not the Lord." When he got a severe disease in his feet, he sought after physicians instead of God. The Bible tells us he slept with his fathers. In other words, he died rather than believe God.

You might say it is difficult to believe God. You might be wondering if you are capable of believing God like you have seen others do. Let me ask you this question: Have you ever thrown a ball into the air? What happens after you throw it up? It comes down. If you throw it up 507 times, it will come down 507 times. Do you know why? It is because there are certain natural laws that remain in effect as long as Earth remains (Genesis 8:22).

Enough Power for a Miracle

Sowing and reaping are part of that law. If we sow the Word in our hearts, we will get a crop. Sow a little, reap a little. A farmer can plant two seeds or a ton of seeds. The sun does not adjust its rays according to how many he plants. There are enough rays being poured down on the Earth to germinate the whole ton. If a farmer decides to plant just two seeds, the sun's rays are still there for the ton.

When you walk up to the altar, the Son of God is there. He is pouring out from the stripes on His back enough healing power for your instant miracle (ton) or a "beginning to mend" (two seeds).

I know you have heard teaching on the fig tree. It dried from the roots up. The manifestation came later. This is true, and another of the miracles I will be sharing about later in this book was based on that principle.

However, I am convinced that the glory of God manifesting as supernatural signs, wonders, and miracles in the Church is not based on God but on us. God did His part 2000 years ago. We are learning to believe and act on what He says and receive our miracle.

As a Church, we have been picturing God giving us a little or a lot, according to our faith, but it is not that way at all. It may seem like splitting hairs, but we are missing miracles by a fine line. We are slightly off in our thinking. God has already given us everything, and we are trying to decide if we want it or not.

We Determine Our Miracle

Sally had been sowing large amounts of "seed" into her heart. She had been watching Gospel Bill videos over and over each day. Believing was as easy to her as breathing. Jacob, you remember, got exactly what he wanted. We determine what we will receive!

When I was about 4 years old, I remember watching my 6-year-old brother play in the rain. He was older and braver than I, and I was not certain I wanted to do that. He was running, laughing, and having a ball while I watched timidly out the window.

One day I decided that my desire to have fun was greater than my fear of the rain. So I closed my eyes, held my nose, and dashed out the front door. I was so surprised how easy it was!

As the rain soaked me to the skin, I was refreshed. All my timidity disappeared. Soon I was running, jumping, and laughing. Then, in complete abandon, I jumped into the drainage ditch by the house, totally immersing myself in water. Bobbing up and down, I laughed hilariously.

Church, the end-time revival is already here! The latter-day outpouring has arrived! Have you? Close your eyes, hold your nose, and dash out from behind closed doors. Get soaked to the skin and recklessly abandon yourself in the glory of God!

[1]Gospel Bill Videos, now named Bill Gunter U.S. Marshall, Willie George Ministries, 10838 East Marshall, Suite 152, Tulsa, OK 74116. Phone 1-800-888-7856

Chapter 3
You're Not Pregnant!

Picture a mother preparing a table for guests. The dining room table is graced by a pressed linen cloth, napkin rings with embroidered napkins, and a lovely floral centerpiece purchased just that morning from the local florist. She has set out her finest china and crystal.

As she glances over her handiwork one last time, she is satisfied it could not look any better. Moments before her guests arrive, her 4-year-old son comes running through the front door. His hair is matted to his face with perspiration. Little black streaks of mud run across his forehead, evidence of an earlier attempt to wipe away the wet hair.

Chubby little hands are clutching a combination of weeds and wildflowers, and he pants with glee, "Look, Mommy, I brought you a present for your table. Won't the people be happy?"

The mother takes the untidy bunch of flowers and weeds. She notices that her son has left globs of dirt on the ones that had been pulled up by the roots. Removing the store-bought bouquet from its vase, she lovingly replaces it with her son's gift of love. "Thank you so much, Honey," she says. Then, returning his crushing hug, she says, "This is the most perfect bouquet I have ever seen!"

Jesus told us to be perfect, even as our Father in heaven is perfect (Matthew 5:48). People have said that means we are to be mature. But did God the Father have to mature? Therefore, to be perfect "even as our Father in heaven is" could not be something we grow into. Others say Jesus cannot return until the Church has gotten all the sin out. At any given hour, if the Church is doing her job, there will be brand-new baby Christians who have a lot to "get out."

I am assuming I am writing to a blood-washed Church who know their spirits have been made perfect, but they are now struggling with certain issues, like working out their souls' salvation (Philippians 2:12).

Another Look at Perfection

I believe we need to take another look at perfection.

Perfection is not the absence of imperfection any more than love is an absence of hate.

If you remove every imperfection in the Church, you still have a far-from-perfect Church; that is, if you are trying to obtain by removal.

It is like trying to add by subtraction. It cannot be done. Perfection is in the eye of the beholder.

The mother in our story was not telling a lie when she said the bouquet was the most beautiful she had ever seen. Why? She was not looking at the condition of the flowers; she was looking at the condition of a heart. Those flowers were a visible manifestation of a heart that loved her.

Two Applications

There are two different applications of the story. The first would be that Jesus sacrificed His life to buy us for the Father. Therefore, the Father views His gift as perfect. He does not look at the condition of the gift; rather, at the heart of the Giver.

In that respect, we are just like the wildflowers. We are fit for the Father's table simply because we are presented to Him as a gift from His Son.

The second application is that now we are sons. The gifts we bring to the Father are now viewed beyond the condition of the gifts to the condition of the heart of the giver. For example, not being able to "carry a tune in a basket" in the natural, you may be standing before the Father singing His praises with a heart overflowing with love.

In the Spirit, you already are perfect, in that you are a son. Now, as your soul magnifies the Lord, you stand completely perfect, as both gift and giver. You are now "complete in Him."

It does not matter if you use the first application or the second. The important thing is that you come into an understanding of how the Father views perfection. It is in this understanding that you can begin to rest in Him, not waiver in claiming His promises, reach out in faith, and grab hold of what has been provided for you.

God Is No Respecter of Persons

As I relate the following incident, bear this in mind: The Father is not a respecter of persons (Acts 10:34). What He has done for me, He will do for you. See yourself as He sees you, and you will not doubt that.

Just after turning 40 years old, I began to experience symptoms of pregnancy. One of my daughters was adopted, but the other four had given me plenty of experience with those symptoms. I had not read any of the Word books on supernatural pregnancies or had any teaching on standing against those symptoms, so my previous pregnancies had been difficult. Everything I had experienced before was there: nausea, weakness, dizziness, and vomiting.

Each day I could see my waistline expanding a little more, but I just could not bring myself to make a doctor's appointment and begin the whole pregnancy scene. Having a sixth child was a welcome thought; I just hated what I had to go through to get that child. My stomach seemed to be too large for the time I calculated I could be pregnant. I began to wonder if my symptoms could be something else.

Alarming Symptoms

One afternoon, I noticed that the spotting I had been experiencing since the onset of this "pregnancy" had turned black. I made a mental note that I really needed to call my gynecologist, because I had been experiencing pain in my abdomen. Still, I just could not face making the call.

That same afternoon, as I was coming out of a drug store, I almost fell off the curb after growing dizzy and blacking out momentarily. The drug store was right beside a doctor's office. I immediately went in and asked if I could be examined and get a pregnancy test. They allowed me to have an appointment when I explained what had just happened outside.

The nurse took the specimen for the test. In the middle of the exam, the doctor said to me, "Well, my dear, I have my hands on either a very large baby or a very large tumor, and your pregnancy test was negative."

The doctor encouraged me to go immediately to the hospital, which was located a block away, and have my husband pack a bag for me and take it there. He said I should check myself in and not waste a moment's time. I had just discovered Word teaching, and I knew an operation would not be God's best.

I told the doctor, "No, I am going to go to my church and be prayed for instead." I explained that the Bible says when believers lay hands on the sick, they shall recover. Then I told him what the Word says about being anointed with oil by the elders of the church: The prayer of faith would heal the sick (Mark 16:18; James 5:14,15).

"I Will Not Be Responsible"

He became very angry! He said I must go to the hospital immediately; I had no choice. I stood firm. He told me, "That thing will be growing, and I will not be responsible for what happens."

After I told him I would come back in a month, he became infuriated at what he considered to be my stupidity, and he refused to allow me to leave until I signed a release stating that he had warned me to go directly to the hospital and that he was relieved of all responsibility for my actions.

After returning home, I called my gynecologist and made an appointment for 30 days from that date. I explained to the nurse the reason, and she heartily encouraged me not to wait to come in. Again, I remained firm. A mildly irritated nurse gave me my appointment.

My next stop was the Wednesday night prayer meeting at church. I simply went forward, had hands laid on me, asked to be anointed with oil, the prayer was made, and I sat down. From that point, I grew sicker! All my symptoms increased in intensity with each passing day.

Lying Symptoms

Each time I experienced a symptom like pain or nausea, I would firmly state aloud, "These are lying symptoms. I choose instead to believe God's Word. God's Word says that by Jesus' stripes I am healed, and I choose to believe God's Word instead of lying symptoms. By Jesus' stripes I am healed." But I grew sicker each day.

Finally, I could barely lift my head or walk. The 30 days had passed, and I felt like I was nearly dead. There was no strength in my body to carry out everyday necessities of child care. I was too sick to drive myself to the doctor. The black spotting had become a daily flow. The nausea and dizziness were now constant.

I must have said my confession aloud hundreds of times. I believed with all my heart that even if they buried me, by Jesus' stripes I was healed.

My daughter Glori came to pick me up for my appointment. She helped me into the doctor's office and as we sat there waiting, my head lay over on her shoulder. I had no strength left to hold it up.

One Last Confession

When the nurse called my name, Glori helped me into the examining room. When I saw the table in front of me, I said aloud one last time, "These are lying symptoms. I choose instead to believe God's Word. God's Word says that by Jesus' stripes I am healed, and I choose to believe God's Word instead of these lying symptoms. By Jesus' stripes I am healed!" Glori helped me onto the table and left the room.

When the doctor entered, I explained what had been happening to me. He began the exam. My thoughts were flooded with the first doctor's words, "That thing will be growing..." I cast down the thought. I closed my eyes and firmly thought, "I choose instead to believe God's Word." My thoughts were broken by the doctor's statement, "Well, I don't know where it is. You're as clean as a whistle."

Joy flooded my heart! I yelled, "Praise God!" A few minutes later, after the doctor had left that room, I hopped off that table with the manifestation of complete healing. I was strong, healthy, and filled with vigor.

Another Perplexed Doctor

A few minutes later, I was in another room with the doctor, sitting across from his desk, relating the whole story to him and rejoicing in the Lord. He stared at me as if I was insane. He hardly said a word. He just kept staring at me. I thanked him and left, giving God praise.

I glanced back over my shoulder and caught a final glimpse of him standing behind his desk in silence as he watched me dance out his door.

I was the one who drove the car home. There was not another sign of spotting from that moment on. I did not feel dizzy, nauseated, or weak ever again. My stomach returned to its normal size. It has been more than 10 years, and I have yet to experience another symptom.

This was what is called "the good fight of faith." It has been said that a good fight is the fight that is won. This fight was won. Victory is sweet. It feels *so* good to win!

On the Highway of Healing

There had been a 30-day space of time from when hands were laid on me to when the manifestation came. Just like travelers on the superhighway of healing in Chapter 1, there were many places to exit away from my healing; but just like the farmer in Chapter 2, I had sown enough Word in my heart that I didn't pay any attention to exit opportunities.

As a result of standing on God's Word, knowing who I am in Christ, holding on to the promises, I received my answer. You can, too.

But if I stop here, I would be selling you short. I had victory, and you can have victory, too. But why wait 30 days for the manifestation? Why not experience the instant, supernatural outpouring of God's glory manifested through healing when we pray?

That type of experience takes the reckless abandon to the Spirit of God mentioned in Chapter 2. Before you will be able to free yourself to that degree, you must ask yourself, "Does this stuff work or not?" That question leads us to Chapter 4.

Chapter 4
Crisis Call

This story starts with a little handmade silk ballerina doll. The Lord impressed me to get my sewing box and make one more doll. As I sat and fashioned pink silk, net, and ribbons with pearls and lace, my mind drifted to the many dolls I had made years before.

Mom had wanted to give a special gift to each of her grandchildren, and I offered to make each a special Christmas creation. That led to 47 other dolls, and doll-making became a passion with me. Then followed the collector books, expensive bisque dolls, and all the other things that go with being consumed by a hobby.

The Lord dealt with my heart that year about my commitment to serve Him, so I put aside doll-making along with other things of the world that were consuming my energies and time. Scraps of materials and notions remained untouched in my sewing box for five years.

"Are you sure that's You, Lord? Do You really want me to make a doll?" Yes, He did. I had no idea why. Each of my children questioned me about the doll during the time it was being stitched, gathered, and glued.

"Who are you making the doll for?"

"I have no idea."

"Well then, why are you making it?"

I could not answer that question, either. I knew my Father's voice, and He commissioned the job. It was growing late in the afternoon. I put the final stitches onto the doll's embroidered face, wrapped her in clear cellophane, placed her above my sewing machine, and rushed to prepare the dinner I was already late in starting.

A Messy Cook

I would like to tell you I was broiling skinless chicken and slicing a crisp, healthy salad, but again I was frying chicken. My family loved fried chicken, mashed potatoes with gravy, peas, and lemon meringue pie. We had that meal at least once a week.

If you've ever fried chicken, you know you need to attend to it the entire time it is cooking. Because I always loved to really get *into* my cooking, my hands were covered with globs of egg batter and flour. I had flour up to my elbows. My shirt was gummy and sticky from using it as a cloth to wipe my hands. What can I say? I was a messy cook.

Sometimes after whipping up one of those country meals, I had flour in my hair and egg on my shoes. I think this came from singing while cooking and trying to crack eggs to a rhythm. My point is that it was probably the most inconvenient time I could possibly receive the telephone call that was to come.

A Crisis Call

"Will you feed our dog for us?" I tried to recognize the voice at the other end of the line. Her sobs were heartbreaking, and I heard someone else crying in the background. Unable to get my bearings about who was talking and what was happening, I didn't have a clue as to who was calling me.

"Who is this? What is wrong?"

The voice on the other end of the line became clearer as my neighbor realized she had to get control of herself. She spoke in short, broken syllables, trying to hold back convulsive sobs as she related her problem.

Sarah was my Jewish neighbor. We lived in the country, and because our houses sat on one-and-a-half acre plots, we were not close neighbors. Several times we had walked to our mail boxes at about the same time and had begun to talk.

Closed to the Gospel?

I had witnessed to Sarah a few times, but she seemed closed to the Gospel. One day I gave her one of the Jewish tracts I developed for my hospital ministry. It deals with the Messiah in fulfilled prophecy. It also deals with the fact that the Messiah was to come before the Temple was destroyed.

I love that little tract! It asks the questions: "If not Him, who? If not then, when or how? The Temple was already destroyed, and we no longer crucify men."

When Sarah had taken the tract, she had not even looked down at it. She stared right in my face and shoved the tract between her pieces of mail. I remember thinking it would probably end up in the trash after she got into the house.

A week later, my daughter Sally went over to baby-sit for them. She arrived a little early. Heather, their 6-year-old daughter, had let Sally in the front door. Sally said Sarah was lying across her bed reading my tract! When she saw Sally, she hastily hid the tract under a pillow. It was encouraging to know she was receiving the truth that Jesus is the Messiah.

Eaten Up With Cancer!

Now Sarah was sobbing the terrible news that Heather was eaten up with cancer! They had just returned from their doctor, who told them X-rays revealed that Heather's entire body cavity was filled with cancer, and the roots were wrapped all around her lungs.

The surgery Heather would need was too radical to be handled in our community, so they were flying her to a hospital in Gainesville. There, doctors would operate to see if there was anything that could be done for her, but they gave her no hope.

The family was waiting for Sarah's Mother to arrive to pick up their younger daughter, and they wanted to know if I would feed their dog while they were in Gainesville. I expressed my sympathy and told Sarah I would be praying for her and that naturally I would feed her dog.

It felt like a giant boulder had dropped into my stomach. My youngest was not much older than Heather, and I couldn't comprehend the pain Sarah must be suffering.

Tears streamed down my cheeks as I began weeping in compassion. I was trying to continue frying the chicken, but I could not see for the flood of tears. Trying to wipe my eyes with the upper part of my arm, I cried out, "Why, God? Why little Heather?"

Our Authority

Then something started rising up from the center of my being. The only way I know how to describe it is it was "holy rage." "Wait a minute!" I thought. I slammed my fork down. "I know why — and I have authority over him!"

I ran over to the sink to wash my hands while yelling for Sally and stating through clenched teeth, "Either this stuff is true or it's not! Either this stuff works or it doesn't!"

When Sally arrived in the kitchen, I handed her the fork and said, "Finish the chicken. I have business to take care of." Sally was filled with questions. She could see I had been crying. "What is happening?" she asked.

"Just wait, Sally," I replied.

I picked up the phone and dialed Sarah's house. The same sobbing voice answered. I blurted out with great authority, "Sarah, this is Cookie (my nickname). I know you think the Messiah is still to come. I'm here to tell you He has already come, and His name is Jesus!" My voice raised a little higher with each word spoken and the authority also increased as I heard my own voice speaking this truth.

"Jesus Will Heal Her!"

"If you will allow me 30 seconds to pray for Heather, I promise you — Jesus will heal her!" There was silence on the other end of the line. I took this to mean Sarah was trying to decide if she was going to allow this or not.

"Please, Sarah, I won't even come in. Just bring her to the front porch. Just 30 seconds, Sarah, and I promise you Jesus will heal her! The Bible says if believers lay hands on the sick, they will recover. Heather will be healed!"

I could barely hear the hesitant, "Well...okay, I guess..." Her voice trailed off as if she was in deep thought. I yelled, "I'll be right there!"

The telephone was beside my sewing machine. I grabbed the doll and ran next door. My heart was pounding with resolve. No sooner had I opened the screen door on the small front porch than Sarah appeared at the front door. Her red-rimmed eyes were half-swollen shut. She was blowing her nose into a hankie while trying to walk. Heather was clutching her around the legs, holding on for dear life, peeking out from behind Sarah at me.

In the background stood her weeping father, while her baby sister was playing on the floor as if nothing was going on.

A Closer Look

I stooped down in front of Heather. "Heather, I have something for you," I said. I began to unwrap the cellophane from the doll. Heather moved ever so slightly out from behind her mother to get a closer look. She wiped away her tears to try to see the doll better.

"Look, Heather. Isn't she pretty? I made her just for you! See the little wand. It has ribbons and pearls. It's for you, Heather." I held the doll just out of her reach.

Her father was crying, her mother was sobbing, and Heather had tears running down her cheeks as she inched forward with one arm outstretched to try to reach the doll.

I let her almost touch it, then reached out while she continued stretching for the doll. I touched her on her rib cage ever so lightly and whispered softly and firmly — softly for Heather's sake, firmly for her mom's sake — "In Jesus' Name, you foul spirit of cancer, I command you to dry up and go away!"

Heather grabbed the doll and pulled it close to her as she went back into hiding behind her mother. Heather and Sarah then backed into the house, closing the door without a word.

One More Doll

I just stood there for a moment. I felt like I was going to explode for joy! I *knew* God had touched Heather. As I ran back to check on Sally and the chicken, my thoughts went in grateful praise to Father God, who had quickened me to make one more doll. He knew who that doll was for and that I would need it to coax a frightened little girl out from behind her mother.

We did feed the dog, and we wondered how little Heather was doing. Two days later, when I came home from the grocery store, my husband told me something that had just happened. He said that Sarah's mother had come running over while he was mowing the lawn. She was screaming, "Cookie did a miracle on Heather! Cookie did a miracle on Heather!" She then told him that when the surgeons operated on Heather, they found something they could not explain.

The entire cancerous mass had shriveled up into a tiny sac attached to the end of one rib. There were no roots around her lungs. There was no cancer in her body cavity. There was no cancer anywhere, except that tiny sac. They could not figure out what had happened between the X-rays and the operation.

Sarah's mother said the doctors had checked every part of her granddaughter's body, and they could not find a single cancer cell. Instead of radical surgery with little hope, they snipped off the tiny sac and, just to be safe, a tiny amount of the end of the rib. They could not accept what had happened and suggested Heather be given chemotherapy just to be safe. The parents needlessly took their advice.

The Messiah Appears!

I quickly called the house and told the grandmother, "Cookie did no miracle; Jesus did the miracle. Give Him the glory." She kept saying she knew it was God.

Sarah called me from the hospital. She related the same story her mother had told us, with one addition: Yeshua had appeared to her in Heather's hospital room! He told her His name was Jesus, and He had healed Heather. She then made Him the Lord of her life!

Several weeks after Heather was healed, a huge box arrived from Heather's grandfather, whom I had not met. The box was stuffed with gifts for my family. We opened package after package of all kinds of little gifts and trinkets that came from the grateful grandparents. Eight years have passed, and Heather is still healed.

Through the years prior to this incident, I had done my best to live my life before this family in the best way possible. If they loaned me a stick of butter, I returned a pound. If I borrowed a cup of sugar, I returned five pounds.

Living in the End Times

I believe we need to live our Christian witness before the unsaved, being careful to witness whenever possible and let our light shine. That has been getting the job done for the last 2000 years, but times have changed. These are the end times!

The world is suffering under the assault of a renegade gangster named Satan, who is ravishing lives because he knows his time is short.

He will entice a fanatical terrorist to blow apart a federal building, fill children with cancer, rip babies apart through abortion, and blaspheme all that is holy. He hates you, he hates your children, and he despises the Church.

It does no good to call the police, militia, or Marines. They can't stop him. You are the only one who can stop him! You are the Church of the living God, and you have been given authority over him!

Is this stuff true or not? Does this stuff work or doesn't it? We need to get these questions settled in our hearts once and for all before we ever experience the glory of God.

Questions To Ask Yourself About Crisis Call

1. Why would the Lord ask someone to put aside an interesting hobby?

But seek ye first the kingdom of God, and his righteousness; and all these things shall be added unto you.

Matthew 6:33

No man that warreth entangleth himself with the affairs of this life; that he may please him who hath chosen him to be a soldier.

2 Timothy 2:4

2. Why had Sarah rejected the Gospel prior to Jesus' revealing Himself to her?

But if our gospel be hid, it is hid to them that are lost:

in whom the god of this world hath blinded the minds of them which believe not, lest the light of the glorious gospel of Christ, who is the image of God, should shine unto them.

2 Corinthians 4:3,4

For I would not, brethren, that ye should be ignorant of this mystery, lest ye should be wise in your own conceits; that blindness in part is happened to Israel, until the fullness of the Gentiles be come in.

Romans 11:25

3. Why did Heather have cancer?

The thief cometh not, but for to steal, and to kill, and to destroy: I am come that they might have life, and that they might have it more abundantly.

John 10:10

4. How do we know that we have authority over the devil?

> **He that believeth and is baptized shall be saved; but he that believeth not shall be damned.**
>
> **And these signs shall follow them that believe; In my name shall they cast out devils; they shall speak with new tongues;**
>
> **They shall take up serpents; and if they drink any deadly thing, it shall not hurt them; they shall lay hands on the sick, and they shall recover.**
>
> **Mark 16:16-18**

5. Why did Sarah's Mother assume it was "Cookie" who "did a miracle on Heather"?

> **And when Peter saw it, he answered unto the people, Ye men of Israel, why marvel ye at this? or why look ye so earnestly on us, as though by our own power or holiness we had made this man to walk?**
>
> **Acts 3:12**

The Authority of the Believer

Genesis 1:26-28; 2:15

Exodus 9:16

Numbers 22:38

Deuteronomy 8:18; 30:9-11

2 Samuel 22:33

1 Chronicles 29:11,12

Esther 9:29

Psalms 8:4-8; 66:3; 68:35; 71:18; 115:16

Proverbs 18:21; 29:2

Ecclesiastes 5:19

Isaiah 40:26,29

Zechariah 4:6

Matthew 7:7,8,29; 8:8-10; 10:1,7,8; 16:17-19; 18:18; 28:18-20

Mark 1:22; 6:7; 9:38-40; 13:34; 16:17,18

Luke 4:36; 9:1; 10:1-9,19,20

John 8:31,32; 14:12-14; 17:22

Acts 1:8; 2:43; 3:6,12,13; 5:12; 6:8; 8:6-8; 9:34,40; 10:38; 14:3,10; 15:12; 28:3-6

Romans 8:14-17,37; 9:17

1 Corinthians 9:18

2 Corinthians 2:14; 10:8; 13:4,10

Ephesians 1:18-22; 2:1-6,10; 3:7,20; 6:10,11

Philippians 4:13

Colossians 1:11-20; 2:10,15

2 Thessalonians 3:9

2 Timothy 1:7,9

Titus 2:15

Hebrews 1:1-4; 2:6-8,14

James 4:7

1 Peter 5:8,9

2 Peter 1:3,4

1 John 2:13; 4:4

Revelation 1:18; 12:11

The Glory of the Stallion

I once heard a preacher say that in the context of the original Hebrew, the glory of a thing is the reality of its true nature. In *Strong's Concordance,* glory is defined as "splendor." So it could be said that the glory of a thing is when it is in its full splendor.

Some years back, when I still went to movies, I saw one entitled "The Man From Snowy River." The stallion in that movie was exquisite. He was in his prime, and different camera angles caught the animal's strong, rippling muscles moving beneath his sleek black coat. His mane was simply gorgeous as it whipped toward the sky when the stallion galloped through snowy woods and a river.

In one scene, the stallion was ridden down a mountain that was about a 90-degree angle. The scene, shot in slow motion, was one of the most breathtaking sights I have ever witnessed!

The beauty of that horse left a permanent impression on my mind. I came out of that theater with a greater appreciation for God's creation. Even now, these many years later, as I write about that stallion, I am stirred with love for God. He has created so many wonderful things, and I am so happy to have seen one of His creatures in such splendor. I witnessed the glory of the stallion.

The Glory of the Rose

My daughter Sally loves roses and has planted many different kinds. She is unable to part with even one of the blooms after they grow limp, so she has dried literally hundreds of these flowers.

When first planted, they are rather unattractive. They look like nothing but crooked sticks with thorns. Then they begin to take root and grow. Soon, little green leaves pop out all over the plant, and eventually some tight little buds appear.

I did not pay much attention to Sally's roses until one day when I was bringing in the groceries. The roses were in full bloom. What a sight to behold! What beauty! The groceries were left on the sidewalk as I knelt down and inspected each rose, drinking in its beauty and fragrance. They were a sight too lovely to pass by.

The rose was in full bloom. The rose was in its glory. The reality of the splendor of the rose grew the more I beheld its beauty.

Keeping the above two examples in mind, let me ask you this question: Could I have grasped the reality of the glorious splendor of the stallion or the rose if my eyes had been closed? No! What if Sally had come to me and said, "Mom, will you come look at my roses?" and I had said, "No, I am not really interested in roses." Would I have missed out on something? Yes!

How Do We Know These Are the End Times?

Jesus is a representative of the glory of God. According to John 14:9,10, Jesus is the manifestation of the true nature of God. In other words, Jesus is, in essence, God in full bloom!

As the rose unfolds its petals, you are able to see the glory of the rose. You do not see the complete glory of the rose until the petals are completely unfolded. Then you see the true nature and beauty of the rose. If you behold it when it is first planted, you certainly have not seen its full beauty. If you behold the plant full of buds, you still have not beheld the glory of the rose. It must be beheld with the secrets it once held inside its closed petals open for all to see for its full glory to be revealed.

Likewise, the Word of God is an unfolding of the glory of God expressing His saving plan for mankind, His love, and His true nature through Jesus, the sweet Rose of Sharon.

To have a real look at the glory of God — to be able to fully drink in the beauty of His glory — there must be a total, complete unfolding or revelation of every last petal. Yet the majority of the Church has decided to close their eyes to a very important part of the Word: the revelation of Jesus Christ found in the Book of Revelation.

People who love God, respect His Word, and desire to know Him better have said, like the fictitious Mom above, "No, I'm not really interested in roses" (Revelation). They have chosen to try to see the glory of Jesus without the full revelation of Him that is available to them.

The first verse of Revelation does not say this book is the revelation of the Antichrist or "666." It says it is the Revelation of Jesus Christ. Verse 3 tells us we are blessed if we read this book. Did you notice that? Blessed! I want to be blessed. I want every last "petal" unfolded. I want to see God's glory!

Earlier in this book, I summarized the Book of Ephesians in seven lines. It would be difficult, to say the least, to try that with the Book of Revelation. What I will do, however, is give you a picture of things you need to know to recognize the urgency of the times in which we live. This will be a picture of your future as well as the world to come. Hopefully, your appetite will be wetted for further investigation; a peeking into the secrets the last "petals" hold.

The Fourth Man

There is a famous sermon I have heard several different men preach. It is called "The Fourth Man." It may not have originated with Oral Roberts, but he was the first one I heard preach it, and I have never heard anyone do it better.

Integrity Praise has even put the sermon to song in its album "God With Us."[2] It describes Jesus in every book in the Bible.

In Genesis	He is the Ram at Abraham's altar.
In Exodus	He is the Passover Lamb.
In Leviticus	He is the High Priest.
In Numbers	He is the Cloud by day and the Pillar by night.
In Deuteronomy	He is the City of our Refuge.
In Joshua	He is the Scarlet Thread from Rahab's window.
In Judges	He is our Judge.
In Ruth	He is our Kinsman Redeemer.
In 1 and 2 Samuel	He is our Trusted Prophet.
In Kings and Chronicles	He is our Reigning King.
In Ezra	He is our Faithful Scribe.
In Nehemiah	He is the Builder of everything that is broken.
In Esther	He is Mordecai sitting faithfully at the gate.
In Job	He is our Redeemer that ever liveth.
In Psalms	He is my Shepherd, and I shall not want.

In Proverbs and Ecclesiastes	He is our Wisdom.
In the Song of Solomon	He is the Beautiful Bridegroom.
In Isaiah	He is the Suffering Servant.
In Jeremiah and Lamentations	It is Jesus who is the Weeping Prophet.
In Ezekiel	He is the Wonderful Four-Faced Man.
In Daniel	He is the *Fourth Man* in the midst of the fiery furnace.
In Hosea	He is my Love that is forever faithful.
In Joel	He baptizes us with the Holy Spirit.
In Amos	He is our Burden-Bearer.
In Obadiah	He is our Savior.
In Jonah	He is the Great Foreign Missionary who takes the Word of God to the whole world.
In Micah	He is the Messenger with beautiful feet.
In Nahum	He is the Avenger.
In Habakkuk	He is the Watchman who is ever praying for revival.
In Zephaniah	He is the Lord mighty to save.
In Haggai	He is the Restorer of our lost heritage.
In Zechariah	He is our Fountain.
In Malachi	He is the Son of Righteousness with healing in His wings.
In Matthew	He is the Christ, the Son of the living God.
In Mark	He is the Miracle-Worker.
In Luke	He is the Son of Man.
In John	He is the Door by which everyone must enter.
In Acts	He is the Shining Light that appears to Saul on the road to Damascus.
In Romans	He is our Justifier.

In 1 Corinthians	He is our Resurrection.
In 2 Corinthians	He is our Sin-Bearer.
In Galatians	He redeems us from the Law.
In Ephesians	He is our Unsearchable Riches.
In Philippians	He supplies our every need.
In Colossians	He is the Fullness of the Godhead Bodily.
In 1 & 2 Thessalonians	He is our Soon-Coming King.
In 1 & 2 Timothy	He is the Mediator between God and man.
In Titus	He is our Blessed Hope.
In Philemon	He is the Friend that sticketh closer than a brother.
In Hebrews	He is the Blood of the Everlasting Covenant.
In James	He is the Lord who heals the sick.
In 1 & 2 Peter	He is the Chief Shepherd.
In 1,2,3 John	It is Jesus who has the tenderness of love.
In Jude	He is the Lord coming with 10,000 of His saints.
And in Revelation	Lift up your eyes, Church, for your Redeemer draweth nigh.

He Is King Of Kings and
Lord Of Lords

Four Cardinal Truths

Lester Sumrall wrote an inspirational book called *Pioneers of Faith* in which he mentioned an interesting fact. When revival came at the turn of the century, the new leaders began to preach these four things: salvation, water baptism, the infilling of the Holy Spirit, and the Second Coming of Jesus Christ.

These four cardinal truths built the Full Gospel Movement on the face of the whole Earth! As I read that fact, I realized that those leaders had simply returned to the basics of the Bible. Paul said in Second Corinthians 11:3:

> **But I fear, lest by any means, as the serpent beguiled Eve through his subtilty, so your minds should be corrupted from the simplicity that is in Christ.**

Simplicity, simplicity, simplicity! I cannot emphasize it enough. You will have the greatest moves of God in your lives and churches as you stick to the simplicity of the Gospel.

When I was in Russia, traveling from church to church training pastors and children's workers in children's ministry, they told me what they had been teaching the children.

To my utter astonishment, not a single church worker told me they taught anything about Jesus' return for His Church. I asked one director why they had not taught this subject, and her reply was, "Oh, we are trying to stick to the most basic and important things." I said, "Honey, this is about as basic and important as you can get!"

Jesus Christ Died

Jesus Christ Is Risen

Jesus Christ Is Coming Again

This is our "blessed hope." When we hold this hope, we purify ourselves, according to First John 3:3. When we hold this hope, we are in a state of watchfulness, according to First Thessalonians 5:4-9. When we hold this hope, we are more likely to witness and share this hope.

Everything we learn in the New Testament about the return of Jesus could be misinterpreted without the tremendous scriptural clarification of the Book of Revelation. It is almost like a camera that is not quite in focus. Few know what the picture is, because there is no sharp definition, and many details are cloudy. The Book of Revelation is the focusing lens to the return of Jesus Christ.

When Will the Rapture Occur?

The following example is not going to be an in-depth study of end times; it is simply a taste of the focusing power of Revelation to New Testament Scripture.

There is much debate in the Body of Christ about whether the Rapture of the Church will come *before* the Tribulation, *midway* through the Tribulation, or *at the end* of the Tribulation. One doctrine even arose called "Kingdom Now." It states that we are going to remain on the Earth and go nowhere.

As I hear preachers digress from sound doctrine, I am reminded of this admonishing from the Word:

> **But though we, or an angel from heaven, preach any other gospel unto you than that which we have preached unto you, let him be accursed.**
>
> **Galatians 1:8**

This Scripture is referring to our not departing from the Gospel of Grace. The lesson to be learned from it is: Stick with truth. The Gospel cannot be changed to suit us. We do not have the freedom to develop our own doctrines and search for supporting Scripture.

The Whole Counsel of the Word

We must instead take the whole counsel of the Word from Genesis to Revelation. Our doctrines are just that — *our* doctrines — if they do not line up with the whole Word of God.

So how do people come up with so many different ideas about the return of Jesus? I believe in many cases they have not taken one important end-time Scripture in Revelation and focused it on other Scriptures in the New Testament.

To show you how people come up with their own ideas about Scripture, we will examine several Scriptures. Then I will give you one scripture from Revelation that totally changes what people have believed about those Scriptures.

1. The following sample Scriptures seem to indicate that the Rapture occurs *after* the Tribulation.

Immediately after the tribulation of those days....

Matthew 24:29

And he shall send his angels with a great sound of a trumpet, and they shall gather together his elect from the four winds, from one end of heaven to the other.

Matthew 24:31

2. This sample Scripture seems to indicate that the Rapture occurs *in the middle* of the Tribulation.

And I heard the man clothed in linen, which was upon the waters of the river, when he held up his right hand and his left hand unto heaven, and swear by him that liveth for ever that it shall be for a time, times, and an half; and when he shall have accomplished to scatter the power of the holy people, all these things shall be finished.

Daniel 12:7

In other words, during this three-and-a-half-year period, the power of the saints will be completely shattered by the forces of the Antichrist.

3. This sample Scripture seems to indicate the "Kingdom Now" position, which is that the wicked will be removed, and believers will remain here on Earth.

The Son of man shall send forth his angels, and they shall gather out of his kingdom all things that offend, and them which do iniquity;

And shall cast them into a furnace of fire: there shall be wailing and gnashing of teeth.

Then shall the righteous shine forth as the sun in the kingdom of their Father. Who hath ears to hear, let him hear.

Matthew 13:41-43

Now let's go to the Book of Revelation. Throughout this book, we are shown over and over again that the wrath of God is being poured out on the ungodly. And all through Scripture, we are told that we, the believers, are not appointed to wrath. (These Scriptures follow at the end of this chapter.)

A Watching Church Caught Up

The whole counsel of the Word shows a watching Church caught up in the clouds and spending seven years with Jesus. We will receive our rewards, enjoy the Marriage Supper of the Lamb, and return with Him in victory.

And I saw heaven opened, and behold a white horse; and he that sat upon him was called Faithful and True, and in righteousness he doth judge and make war.

His eyes were a flame of fire, and on his head were many crowns; and he had a name written, that no man knew, but he himself.

And he was clothed with a vesture dipped in blood: and his name is called The Word of God.

And the armies which were in heaven followed him upon white horses, clothed in fine linen, white and clean.

And out of his mouth goeth a sharp sword, that with it he should smite the nations: and he shall rule them with a rod of iron: and he treadeth the winepress of the fierceness and wrath of Almighty God.

And he hath on his vesture and on his thigh a name written, KING OF KINGS, AND LORD OF LORDS.

Revelation 19:11-16

If we take the *first scripture* that seemed to make a case for a post-Tribulation Rapture and shine the above passage from Revelation on it, we have a problem. How can the saints be on the Earth to be gathered by the angels?

The above Scripture shows that we are arriving on Earth with Jesus, and it shows we were in heaven. If we were in heaven, who are the elect who are gathered?

A Flawed Theory

So you say to yourself, "This looks like there is something wrong with my theory. I wonder what the truth of the Word is?" Your next step would be to begin to ask, seek, and knock. God will show you. The important thing is not to cling to doctrine that the Word has shown to be wrong.

I have observed that sometimes people are afraid to let go of one thing until they have something else to hold on to. I believe that as you continue to study, you will find that the elect of our first Scripture are the *Jewish* elect who will be on Earth while the Church and all other raptured saints will be in heaven.

The *second Scripture* suffers from much the same problem, because our Revelation Scripture shows members of the Church already possessing their "fine linen, white and clean." These garments are part of the rewards of the Christian.

How can the Church be on Earth and be raptured in the *middle of the Tribulation*, when by the middle of the Tribulation, she has already been at the Judgment Seat of Christ and has received her rewards?

Finally, what about our *third example*, that shows the wicked are the ones who are gathered out instead of the Church? If I held to this theory and then came across our Revelation Scripture, I would be forced to say, "If the saints are coming back with Jesus, they must have been gathered to Him previous to the gathering of the wicked."

As you study further, you will find if you back up and focus on Matthew 13:40, you will see that it is referring to "the end of this world." That is a totally different time frame from our Rapture Scriptures.

Line Up With Scripture

The most important thing of all is to be willing to lay aside what we have been taught, what we believe to be true, and what we feel secure in if Scripture shows it to be incorrect. God is so faithful. He does not want us groping around in the dark. He wants us to understand, and He will give us wisdom if we ask Him for it.

Your Revelation studies will further show you prophecies unfolding in the daily newspapers. Israel's becoming a nation again in 1948 was the final birth pain that has moved the world to the transition part of labor, and now birth is imminent!

No other generation previous to this one has had the technology in place to fulfill all remaining Bible prophecies. These are exciting times! These are the end times!

After the return of Jesus to Earth with the Church, His feet will split the Mount of Olives when He steps onto it, He will slay the wicked with the breath of His mouth, Satan will be bound for a thousand years, and we will spend the next thousand years with Him in His Millennial Kingdom. Isn't the Gospel *good news?*

After a thousand years, Satan will be loosed. Death and hell will deliver up their dead. We will experience the Great White Throne Judgment. Satan, wicked angels, and wicked men will be thrown into the Lake of Fire.

Heavenly Jerusalem

The Earth will melt, and we will get a new heaven and a new Earth. That heavenly city, which is built foursquare, will descend to Earth, and God will dwell with us forever!

And I saw a new heaven and a new earth: for the first heaven and the first earth were passed away; and there was no more sea.

And I John saw the holy city, new Jerusalem, coming down from God out of heaven, prepared as a bride adorned for her husband.

And I heard a great voice out of heaven saying, Behold, the tabernacle of God is with men, and he will dwell with them, and they shall be his people, and God himself shall be with them, and be their God.

And God shall wipe away all tears from their eyes; and there shall be no more death, neither sorrow, nor crying, neither shall there be any more pain: for the former things are passed away.

Revelation 21:1-4

What an awesome peek into the center petals unfolding, revealing the glory of the Father and the Son. Then we see Jesus Himself closing the final chapter of Revelation with encouragement regarding the authorship of these letters to the churches.

> **I Jesus have sent mine angel to testify unto you these things in the churches. I am the root and the offspring of David, and the bright and morning star.**
>
> **And the Spirit and the bride say, Come. And let him that heareth say, Come. And let him that is a thirst come. And whosoever will, let him take the water of life freely**
>
> **Revelation 22:16,17**

Sample Scriptures Showing End-Time Events

Jesus Is Coming Again

John 14:1-3

Luke 21:28

1 Corinthians 15:51-58

Jesus will first come for the Church, meeting believers in the air. This is a time of comfort and joy for the Church. His feet will not touch the Earth. This is called the Rapture.

The Rapture

Acts 1:11

1 Thessalonians 1:9,10

1 Thessalonians 4:13-18

1 Thessalonians 5:1-6,9

2 Thessalonians 2:1-8

Philippians 3:20,21

Colossians 3:4

The Church Is Not Appointed to Wrath

Luke 21:34-36

1 Thessalonians 5:9

Revelation 3:10

We will then be judged for our works, whether they are good or bad. This is where the Church receives her rewards. This is called:

The Judgment Seat of Christ

Romans 14:10

1 Corinthians 3:13-15

2 Corinthians 5:10

Fig Tree Tied to End-Time Events

Matthew 24:29-34

Mark 13:24-30

Luke 21:29-32

The Marriage Supper of the Lamb

Luke 14:24

Revelation 19:7-9

After the Rapture, the Judgment Seat of Christ, and the Marriage Supper of the Lamb, we will return to Earth with Him. This is not a time of comfort for the ungodly; instead, it is a day of vengeance. This time, unlike the Rapture, His feet touch the Earth and split the Mount of Olives. This is:

The Second Coming of Christ

2 Thessalonians 1:7,8,10

Jude 14,15

Revelation 1:7; 19:14; 11-21

His Feet Split The Mount of Olives, and He Slays the Wicked With the Breath of His Mouth

Isaiah 11:4

Zechariah 12:10,11; 14:1-5,9

[2]Integrity Praise, etc. Used with permission. Integrity music print license number 9451-4012-PR-1.

Part 2

The Glory of God Manifested Through Healing and Provision

Chapter 5
Adam, Where Art Thou?

When my children were younger, I discovered the promises of the overcomer in the Book of Revelation. These are some of the most exciting promises in the Word. Let's look at them.

> **He that hath an ear, let him hear what the Spirit saith unto the churches; To him that overcometh will I give to eat of the tree of life, which is in the midst of the paradise of God.**
>
> **Revelation 2:7**

I was still a baby Christian at the time. Notice I did not say a "new" Christian. There is a difference. You can become a new Christian and remain a baby for years!

Some people never leave this stage. They will sit at the same table with us, enjoying the Marriage Supper of the Lamb. They will receive rewards for the precious deeds done for Jesus that they did out of a heart of love.

The difference between a *baby* Christian and a *mature* Christian is that a baby is unskilled in the Word of righteousness. In other words, they do not fully understand who they are in Christ Jesus. Consequently, the devil walks all over them in the area of sickness and disease, finances, and so forth.

> **For every one that useth milk is unskillful in the word of righteousness: for he is a babe.**
>
> **But strong meat belongeth to them that are of full age, even those who by reason of use have their senses exercised to discern both good and evil.**
>
> **Hebrews 5:13,14**

To grow past babyhood, you need to "drink" all your spiritual milk, the Word, personalize it — make it your own — and then go on to strong meat. Notice that the Revelation Scriptures said, "He that hath an ear, let him hear."

Essentially, that means to really hear with understanding, making the truth your own. Does it go into your physical ears, through your spiritual ears, drop from your head into your heart, and become revelation knowledge that transforms your life?

Enticing Scriptures

When I read the "overcoming" Scriptures from Revelation 2:7, they sounded exciting. This one was especially enticing. Jesus Christ was going to be giving me to eat of the tree of life!

At that time, our mealtimes consisted of my cutting plates of food into small pieces for the children, pouring beverages, serving, wiping spills, and so forth. Remember, there was a lot of messy cooking that took place first.

This promise sounded wonderful! *I* was the one who was going to be served, and it was going to take place in the midst of the paradise of God. I had no idea where the tree or the garden were. All I knew was that wherever it was, it must be air-conditioned. How else could it be a paradise? And I was not going to have to cook! That was good enough for me. It made me want to become an overcomer.

Escaping Death

The second promise of the overcomer was about escaping death. Who wants to die? This also sounded good to me.

> **He that hath an ear, let him hear what the Spirit saith unto the churches; He that overcometh shall not be hurt of the second death.**
>
> **Revelation 2:11**

The third promise said:

> **He that hath an ear, let him hear what the Spirit saith unto the churches; To him that overcometh will I give to eat**

of the hidden manna, and will give him a white stone, and in the stone a new name written, which no man knoweth saving he that receiveth it.

Revelation 2:17

Scholars say the white stone has something to do with the pronouncing of innocence on one judged, but I had yet to discover that fact. I just started trying to figure out what good a name would be if no man knew it but the one who received it.

Meditating on the Scripture, I pictured a crowd of millions before the throne. The Holy One calls out a name. It is your name. Of the millions standing there, you are the only one who can answer, "Here I am, Lord!" Wow! I wanted that promise. It put a strong desire in my heart to be an overcomer.

The fourth and fifth promises are:

And he that overcometh, and keepeth my works unto the end, to him will I give power over the nations:

And he shall rule them with a rod of iron; as the vessels of a potter shall they be broken to shivers: even as I received of my Father.

And I will give him the morning star.

He that hath an ear, let him hear what the Spirit saith unto the churches.

Revelation 2:26-29

Power over nations was a little beyond my ability to visualize. I would settle for power over a dirty house! The morning star stood for Jesus, and this promise said He would be mine. That was promise enough for me. These promises were getting better all the time!

Promises six and seven were equally exciting:

He that overcometh, the same shall be clothed in white raiment; and I will not blot out his name out of the book of life, but I will confess his name before my Father, and before his angels.

He that hath an ear, let him hear what the Spirit saith unto the churches.

Revelation 3:5,6

Having small children, wearing white was a luxury reserved for special nights out alone with my husband. An all-white dress would not last five minutes with sticky little fingers, drool, and diaper changes. White raiment meant dressing for a special occasion.

Worth Enlisting

Then the seventh promise showed that God Himself would know me. This was a great revelation! Six and seven were definitely worth enlisting in the battle to become an overcomer.

Behold, I come quickly: hold that fast which thou hast, that no man take thy crown.

Him that overcometh will I make a pillar in the temple of my God, and he shall go no more out: and I will write upon him the name of my God, and the name of the city of God, which is new Jerusalem, which cometh down out of heaven from my God: and I will write upon him my new name.

Revelation 3:11,12

The part of the eighth and ninth promises that stood out to me was the phrase "no more out." The struggle against sin had been a major part of my life up to this point. There seemed to be a revolving door to the Throne Room. Go in and get forgiveness. Go out and sin. Go back in and get forgiveness — and on and on.

The thought of going in and *staying* there sounded like a rest that would be well worth the struggle. Oh, to be free! I wanted it.

A Promise of Honor

The tenth Scripture was a promise of honor.

To him that overcometh will I grant to sit with me in my throne, even as I also overcame, and am set down with my Father in his throne.

Revelation 3:21

There did not seem to be much honor from the world for being a good mother. After walking the floor all night with a crying baby, doing several loads of laundry, ironing, cooking, washing dishes, cleaning house, refereeing arguments, kissing boo-boos, giving baths, and tucking little ones in bed, I would collapse into a chair, thinking there should be some special award for mothers.

It should be made out of solid gold with silver letters that say, "In Appreciation." I would pin it to my dress for all to see. When I walked down the street, people would look admiringly at the medal and say with awe and deep respect, "Oh, look. She's a mother!"

But no honor came. In fact, it was just the opposite. Once it was discovered that I did not "work," and I was "just a housewife," new acquaintances would begin to choose smaller words as they spoke to me, to be certain I would understand what they were saying. Promise 10 would give me honor. Now I was *determined* to overcome, no matter what else I accomplished.

The Best of All

Promises 11 and 12 were the best of all!

> **He that overcometh shall inherit all things; and I will be his God, and he shall be my son.**
>
> **Revelation 21:7**

"All things" is a lot to inherit. And God was "choosing" to be my God. He was not putting up with me just because I happened to be one of the "fish" in the net. He was choosing me personally. I loved the fact that He would be "my" God.

I discovered these 12 promises the day before our church's annual Hallelujah Party was held in lieu of Halloween. Each of us was to come dressed as someone from the Bible.

One of my daughters dressed as Mary, the mother of Jesus; another as a bunny from Noah's Ark. One of my sons wore "the armor of God," and the other went as a raven that fed the prophet Elijah.

The Overcomer

Excitedly, I adorned myself as an overcomer, wearing a white robe and gold crown. Twelve gold badges were pinned across the front of the robe, each representing a promise.

One badge had a white stone glued in the center of it. Another was decorated with a piece of wheat representing "hidden manna," and written beneath it were the words "I will give you to eat of the hidden manna." Each badge had the promise written, but none said the promise was for being an overcomer.

It was quite obvious from the pastor's fishing pole, overalls, rubber boots, and fish bucket that he had come as a fisher of men.

Each party-goer's identity was guessed quickly — except mine. No one could guess who I was in the Bible. They stood in front of me, reading the promises off my badges, but no one could figure out the answer.

It was such fun! I would laugh, "Come on, now. Don't tell me you don't know who I am. You read your Bible, don't you?" Person after person read the promises, but no one knew who was to receive them! How proud I felt that no one there knew their Bible quite as well as I.

Who Was I?

The evening came to a close. A small group gathered around me. It was time to reveal my identity. Who was I? Standing speechless in front of them, I realized to my horror that I had forgotten who I was! Quickly, I read the promises on my chest. What was I supposed to do to get these promises? I could not remember!

Everyone had a big laugh, and I went home very humbled. As I was driving home, my kids were laughing and eating candy. I was sitting there talking to myself. "Who am I? I knew when I left the house, but somehow I have forgotten. I know, I know who I am... Oh yes, I remember now. *I'm an overcomer!"*

I had spent so much time focusing on the *rewards* that I had forgotten what my Father desired from me. He desired that I overcome. To overcome, you have to have something to overcome. To have victory, there must be something to have victory over.

You cannot win a war if there is no war. For years I homeschooled my children. Teaching sentence structure using the sentence "Go," I would explain that "Go" is a sentence because the word "you" is the understood subject. It really means, "You go."

Overcoming the Devil

In all the promises of the overcomer there is a something understood though not mentioned directly. That something or someone is the devil whom we must overcome, and we have been given the tools to do exactly that.

> **And they overcame him by the blood of the Lamb, and by the word of their testimony; and they loved not their lives unto the death.**
>
> **Revelation 12:11**

In Genesis, we find something quite interesting about the creation of man:

> **So God created man in his own image, in the image of God created he him; male and female created he them.**
>
> **And God blessed them, and God said unto them, Be fruitful, and multiply, and replenish the earth, and subdue it: and have dominion over the fish of the sea, and over the fowl of the air, and over every living thing that moveth upon the earth.**
>
> **Genesis 1:27,28**

Subdue the Earth

God no sooner had created man than the first thing He spoke to Adam was the instruction to subdue the Earth and all its creatures. *Subdue?* The Garden of Eden was perfect. The animals were already peaceful. In fact, in Genesis 2:19,

God brought all the animals to Adam so he could name them. Why, then, should God tell him to subdue the Earth?

The first words from God's mouth to Adam were actually a prophetic commandment blessing. The Hebrew word for "subdue" is *kabash,* which means "to tread down, disregard, conquer." God was telling man that he was going to have something to subdue. A rebellious renegade was going to enter the garden and bring destruction, disease, and death with him.

Animals would turn on each other as well as the man if man did not subdue the renegade. Adam did not use the authority that was given to him. God had blessed him with this authority as a birth blessing, yet he cast it aside as an unwanted, unneeded tool.

Instead, Adam obeyed the evil one and disobeyed God's command to subdue. In essence, Adam took the badge of authority God had pinned on him, and he pinned it on the devil, giving him dominion over the Earth.

God's Mercy to Mankind

When the Lord God called to Adam and asked, "Where art thou," God was not asking Adam which tree he was hiding behind. God knew exactly where Adam was, because He is God. He was simply pointing out to Adam, "Look where you are. You laid down your authority."

Also notice God did not strike Adam with lightning. Instead, He lovingly prepared a covering of skins, shedding an innocent animal's blood as a type and shadow of the redemption He already had prepared for mankind.

Then, as a further act of love, God removed Adam and Eve from the garden, lest they eat of the tree of life and live forever in a state of unrighteousness. He even placed cherubims to guard the entrance to be certain Adam and Eve were protected from eternal damnation while He brought about His plan of redemption in the Earth.

Now He goes even further in His bountiful mercy toward mankind. Instead of saying, "See if I ever trust you with authority again," He comes to Earth as His own Son, suffers terrible agony to purchase us back, and not only gives us back our lost authority, but adds to it!

The Power To Overcome

In the garden, man only had the ability to *subdue,* but through Jesus' death, burial, and resurrection, we now have the ability to *overcome.* The Greek word for "overcome" is *nikao.* It not only means everything the Hebrew word "subdue" means, but it carries the additional meaning "prevail and get the victory." The dictionary meaning of "prevail" is "to be stronger; win the victory; succeed."

"Victory" carries a note of finality with it, being:

> the defeat of an enemy in combat, battle, or war, the advantage or superiority gained in defeating the enemy or an opponent in battle; triumph gained by force of arms; success in any contest, struggle, or enterprise; supremacy, superiority, or triumph in any effort.

A glorious Church is a victorious Church. A glorious Church is a triumphant Church which has not only subdued but overcome the evil one.

> **Even the mystery which hath been hid from ages and from generations, but now is made manifest to his saints:**
>
> **To whom God would make known what is the riches of the glory of this mystery among the Gentiles; which is Christ in you, the hope of glory.**
>
> **Colossians 1:26,27**

Think about that for a moment! God not only gives back everything and more; He goes further still, saying, "I am even going to indwell you and *do it for you."* Christ in you, the Bible says. We are His purchased possession.

Summarizing the Vision

When the Lord told me to write my vision and calling on paper, it was quite extensive. He then told me to summarize it, to summarize it again, and then summarize it again. Finally, several pages were brought down to these three objectives:

Preach the Blood

Win Souls

Know God

The Gospel is very simple. We have many weapons for battle, but ultimately we will win through:

The Blood of the Lamb

The Word of Our Testimony

(Revelation 12:11)

Let's look at the subject of the blood for a moment. Blood is made up of different properties.

The red blood cells carry oxygen. They are produced in the bone marrow, the living tissue in the center of certain bones. The white cells engulf and devour bacteria and promote healing of injuries.

Platelets gather where a blood vessel is injured and form a plug across the opening, dying in the process. These cells circulate in the blood's liquid component blood plasma.[3]

Life Is in the Blood

No wonder Leviticus 17:11 tells us that the life of the flesh is in the blood! When Jesus poured out His blood, He was pouring out His life for us, that we might overcome.

We must partake of that life and partake of the healing properties as well as its oxygen-giving properties — His breath, filling us with His Spirit.

His blood has many other benefits. They are: the Name of Jesus, the power of binding and loosing, spiritual armor, and so forth. We reach out and take what that blood offers, and then declare it.

Otherwise, we end up like I did at the Hallelujah Party: To our horror, we realize that we do not know who we are! We knew earlier when we were digging into the Word. In fact, we were pretty fired up about it, but as soon as we got out in a traffic jam or someone cut in front of us and took the last parking spot, we forget who we are.

We knew when we left the house, but the reality stayed back home with our Bible and colored markers. We must declare aloud, lest we forget:

> **Speaking to yourselves in psalms and hymns and spiritual songs, singing and making melody in your heart to the Lord.**
>
> **Ephesians 5:19**

Budget Problems

When I first started reading the Bible, God began to make Himself known to me. He had miraculously given me a house. I was raising my little girl alone. The week we moved in, I sat down and figured out a budget. There was money for everything but food!

I prayed, asking God what to do. The Lord gave me the answer: "Tithe." I explained to God that He did not understand. I was trying to get *more* money coming in, not pay out more money. Again He said, "Tithe." This happened three times.

I'd had no teaching on tithing other than bits and pieces, hearing my grandpa mention it. Although I could not understand it, I was afraid *not* to obey. My tithe was $9.28. I wrote the check to a TV ministry because I was in a traditional religious church and had no idea how to go about tithing. The check was in my purse.

That afternoon, I had a doctor's appointment for my daughter, Glori. She had 110 warts across her knuckles and knees! She was almost 9 years old, and the warts were very embarrassing to her. In addition, as she played they were continually being bumped and made to bleed.

A Bad Report

The doctor gave me some distressing news. These warts were the type that had roots. He would only be able to remove three each week, and the cost of each visit would be

$35, which was a lot of money 23 years ago. He added that if she continued to hit them and make them bleed, they could even turn cancerous.

A blanket of despair covered me as I drove away from his office. Where could I possibly get another $35 each week? It was impossible! Satan immediately reminded me of the tithe money in my purse. Now I would be forced to keep the tithe. I would have no choice.

As we drove home, the battle raged between flesh and spirit. Naturally, I did not recognize that fact. I thought I was just reasoning what I should do.

One thing I have learned over the years is to obey God. He taught me this many times. Doing what He showed me always brought great rewards. Disobeying, reasoning that the inward witness was just my own thoughts, always caused much grief.

Listen and Obey

The Spirit of God is always there trying to warn us when we are about to make a wrong decision. We just need to learn to listen and obey.

I spotted a mailbox a block or so down the road. I pulled over quickly and put the tithe in the mail before I could change my mind. Knowing that my only bridge was now burned, small though it was, I laid hands on Glori's knees and cried out to God in the Name of Jesus.

Not knowing the correct words to use or the proper way to bind the enemy, I said with my whole heart, "Father, You will just have to handle these warts. There is nothing else I can do. Thank You for doing it. In Jesus' Name."

A short time later, we pulled into our driveway. Mail was sticking out of the top of the mailbox on the door. My tithing miracle was in that box.

A friend I had not seen in several years had mailed me three times the amount of my tithe check! Plus, her letter said God had instructed her to do this, and she would continue until He told her to stop. Her checks came faithfully for almost two years. The very week I no longer needed the money, the checks quit arriving.

Waking Up to a Miracle

The next morning, I walked into Glori's room to wake her for school. She was asleep on her side with her hands tucked beneath her pillow. I reached forward, pulling her hands out from under the pillow.

"Come on, Sweetie. Time to get up." As her hands appeared, there were snow white scars across all her fingers! The spots looked like the untanned skin under your bathing suit strap after several full days of tanning. As I stood there dumbstruck, it felt like my heart had stopped beating.

I threw the covers down, and there were her knees in exactly the same condition! Don't ask me why I did this, but I started feeling all over the sheets for the warts. There was nothing in that bed except a miracle — a little girl who had been covered with disgusting and painful warts was now clean and new!

My voice returned, and I began to scream, jump, and dance while praising the Lord. An extremely happy little girl went to school that day.

I had accidentally received a miracle! The accident was on my part, not God's. Stumbling blindly into a spiritual law, I had used the Name of Jesus and believed that I received when I prayed.

> **Therefore I say unto you, What things soever ye desire, when ye pray, believe that ye receive them, and ye shall have them.**
>
> **Mark 11:24**

The "eyes of my understanding" had suddenly become enlightened.

> **That the God of our Lord Jesus Christ, the Father of glory, may give unto you the spirit of wisdom and revelation in the knowledge of him:**

The eyes of your understanding being enlightened; that ye may know what is the hope of his calling, and what the riches of the glory of his inheritance in the saints.

Ephesians 1:17,18

Just as God had asked, "Adam, where art thou?" in the *negative* sense, He was calling me to attention with the same question in a *positive* sense.

The natural warts had been removed with nothing left behind save clean, baby-like skin. The spiritual warts or scales had fallen off my eyes, leaving in their place a new, clean understanding of my Father. He loved me, desired to show me His glory, and was just waiting for me to call on Him so He could answer.

The Spiritual Battle

Returning to the point where I was driving home from the doctor's office, remember the spiritual battle that was raging between my flesh and my spirit? This is where the overcoming part comes in.

Suppose for a moment that I had not overcome the lies of the devil. I would have operated in fear, kept the $9.28, and that would have been my source. My next step would have been to try to figure out where to get another $25.72 to make the $35 I needed for the next doctor's appointment.

By quickly mailing the check, I had overcome the devil and entered into the law of sowing and reaping. No longer was the $9.28 my source. By giving into the kingdom of God, all the resources of the kingdom were mine!

Give, and it shall be given unto you; good measure, pressed down, and shaken together, and running over, shall men give into your bosom. For with the same measure that ye mete withal it shall be measured to you again.

Luke 6:38

You might say, "Wait a minute! You didn't give a very big measure." True, looking at it through the eyes of man, $9.28 is not a lot of money. The key here, however, is that it was all that was standing between me and obedience.

Giving My All

The devil was telling me the lie that it was my only resource. By giving it anyway, I was giving my all. In my mind, it was a very big measure. What the devil had not planned on by convincing me my situation was desperate was that my prayer would then of necessity become very fervent!

Here we have yet another spiritual law. Every promise in the Word of God is true. One of those promises is:

> **...The effectual fervent prayer of a righteous man availeth much.**
>
> **James 5:16**

No matter which way the devil turns, he loses. We have called him devil, Satan, slewfoot, and serpent. It is time we began to call him *Defeated!*

We have called ourselves tired, lonely, sick, depressed, and beaten down. It is time to call ourselves by the following names, answering the question, "Where art thou?"

I am in Him	Ephesians 10
I am chosen	1 Thessalonians 1:4
I am born of the incorruptible seed of the Word	1 Peter 1:23
I am forgiven	Ephesians 1:7
I am a new creature	2 Corinthians 5:17
I am the temple of the Holy Spirit	1 Corinthians 6:19
I am delivered from darkness and transformed into God's kingdom	Colossians 1:13
I am redeemed from the curse of the law	Galatians 3:13
I am strong in the Lord	Ephesians 6:10
I am without blame and holy before Him	Ephesians 1:4
I am accepted in Christ	Ephesians 1:6
I am blessed	Deuteronomy 28:1-14
I am a saint	Romans 1:7

I am qualified to share in His inheritance	Colossians 1:12
I am the head and not the tail	Deuteronomy 20:13
I am above only and not beneath	Deuteronomy 28:13
I am victorious	Revelation 21:7
I am dead to sin	Romans 6:2,11
I am elect	Colossians 3:12
I am loved with an everlasting love	Jeremiah 31:3
I am free	John 8:31-33
I am crucified with Christ	Galatians 2:20
I am alive with Christ	Ephesians 2:5
I am raised up with Christ and seated with Him in heavenly places	Colossians 2:12
I am salt and light	Matthew 5:13,14
I am called of God	2 Timothy 1:9
I am more than a conqueror	Romans 8:37
I am an ambassador for Christ	2 Corinthians 5:20
I am beloved of God	1 Thessalonians 1:4
I am born of God	1 John 5:18
I am a king and priest unto God	Revelation 1:6
I am a joint heir with Christ	Romans 8:17
I am reconciled to God	2 Corinthians 5:18
I am healed	1 Peter 2:24
I am a fellow citizen with the saints of the household of God	Ephesians 2:19
I am sealed with the promise of the Holy Spirit	Ephesians 1:13

I am complete in Christ	Colossians 2:10
I am the apple of my Father's eye	Psalm 17:8
I am free from condemnation	Romans 8:1
I am the righteousness of God through Jesus Christ	2 Corinthians 5:21
I am firmly rooted, built up, strengthened in the faith and overflowing with thankfulness	Colossians 2:7
I am a disciple of Christ because I have love for others	John 13:34,35
I am built on the foundation of the apostles and prophets, with Christ Jesus Himself as the Chief Cornerstone	Ephesians 2:20
I am a partaker of His divine nature	2 Peter 1:4
I am God's workmanship, created in Christ Jesus for good works	Ephesians 2:10
I am being changed into His image	Philippians 1:6
I am one in Christ	John 17:21-23
I am empowered to lay hands on the sick and see them recover	Matthew 16:17
I am filled with peace	Philippians 4:7
I am filled with abundant life	John 10:10
I am able to do all things through Christ	Philippians 4:13

I am walking in Christ Jesus	Colossians 2:6
I am filled with the Greater One	1 John 4:4
I am always triumphing in Christ	2 Corinthians 2:14
I am an *Overcomer*	Revelation 12:11
Christ is in me the Hope of Glory!	Colossians 1:27

[3]*Understanding Science and Nature/Human Body.* Alexandria, Virginia: Time-Life.

Chapter 6
God's Service Station

Everyone thought my mother was being quite extravagant when she gave my little brother three names. Earl Stuart Howard Burman cooed, yawned, and slept unaware of the legacy of character hoped to be passed to him through those names.

Stuart was my mother's cunning brother, able to fall in the mud and come up smelling like a rose. Everything he touched turned to gold. Howard was her other brother, who always came to her rescue when anyone tried to hurt her. She would tell me how safe she felt knowing she could call on him when needed.

Earl was her father, Grandpa to me, who loved the Lord with all his heart. In all my growing-up years, I never saw Grandpa leave the house without first kneeling at the door, hat in hand, and give thanks to the Lord for going with him.

Upon returning, he always knelt again, thanking the Lord that He had been with him while away. I imagine that Mother looked into her little child's face and thought, "I desire for you to prosper like Stuart, to love like Howard, and to be wholly separated unto God like Earl."

Names are very important. Names are always given by others — given by those responsible for care — and received by those who have no choice as to what their name will be. Sometimes names are an accurate prediction of what the individual's character will be. At other times, we can see no resemblance between the name and the reputation of the recipient. Knowing this to be true, we often become less sensitive to the tremendous power that lies behind the names of God.

The Names of God

Yes, we know His name Jehovah-Jireh means "the Lord Will Provide," and we think, "I hope He will do that." Did you ever stop to think that God was both the giver and the recipient of His names? He had both the ability to know His own nature and to name Himself for our benefit.

He is omnipotent and omniscient — in other words, all-powerful, almighty, all-seeing, and all-knowing. The Lord knew precisely what He was doing naming Himself. [4]

Yahweh-Jehovah	"I AM the Lord"
Jehovah-Elohim	The Lord Is God
Jehovah-Elyon	The Lord God Most High
El-Shaddai	The Almighty God
Jehovah-Jireh	The Lord Will Provide
Jehovah-Repheka	The Lord Is Healer
Jehovah-Tsidqenu	The Lord Is Our Righteousness
Jehovah-Tsebaoth	The Lord of Hosts
Jehovah-Nissi	The Lord My Banner
Jehovah-Shalom	The Lord Is Peace
Jehovah-Shamah	The Lord Is There

In the Book of Daniel, God is called the Ancient of Days [5] (venerable, Lord most vehement, sacred name, continually daily). Daniel 7:9 describes Him as wearing garments as white as snow, having hair like pure wool, and sitting on a fiery throne.

In the Person of Jesus, He is called: [6]

Messiah

Lord

Master

Truth

Day Star

Prince of Peace
The Way
Fortress
Mighty God
King of Kings
Savior
Shepherd
Rock of Ages
Word of Life
Holy One
Cornerstone
Lion of Judah
Son of David
Light of the World
Lord of All
Holy Lord of Glory
King of the Ages
Righteous Judge
Head of the Church
Son of Righteousness
Morning Star
Lord God Almighty
Lamb of God
Alpha and Omega
Redeemer
Lily of the Valley

In the Person of the precious Holy Spirit, He is called: [7]

Comforter
Counselor
Spirit of Truth
Advocate
Friend

Leader
Intercessor
Guide
Partner
Standby
Strengthener
Helper
Teacher
Paraclete
The Spirit of God
The Spirit of the Lord
The Spirit of the Living God
The Spirit of Christ
The Spirit of the Father
The Holy Spirit of God
The Spirit of Jesus Christ
The Eternal Spirit
The Spirit of Wisdom and Revelation
The Spirit of Knowledge
The Spirit of Counsel and Might
The Spirit of Grace and Supplication
The Breath of the Almighty
The Power of the Highest
The Spirit of Holiness
The Spirit of Love
The Spirit of Truth
The Spirit of Life
The Spirit of Faith
The Spirit of Grace
The Spirit of Power
The Spirit of Prophecy
The Unction and Anointing
The Spirit of Glory

If my brother's three names seemed a lot to live up to, what do you think about these 80 names of God? This is not an all-inclusive list, either. But the most important thing to bear in mind is that God is not trying to live up to these names. They are just a few infinitesimal descriptions of the non-changing character of our Father.

The Character of God

The Lord never has to ask us to forgive Him for getting out of love with us. He is love. He never says we have to wait while He searches around for some more truth in order to give us revelation knowledge on a subject. He did not grow into the names. He has always been what His names say He is. He is today what His names say He is, and He will be thus tomorrow and forever. He is God.

Once it has been settled in our hearts that He is everything He says He is, we need to realize He is everything He says He is for us alone.

We seem to understand that God is watching over His Body of believers. When we squeeze into that holy crowd, we are surrounded by the best. The Body is like a huge freight train streaming across the land. It is being pulled by a strong engine (Jesus) as the Head and is fueled by burning coal (the Holy Spirit).

Thundering down previously laid tracks (God's direction), we know that although it will slow down at times and even stop at stations so others can board, it will eventually arrive at its destination.

A Personal Relationship With God

So the real question is not if we believe God watches over His Body, of which we are a part; the question we must answer is whether we believe God is watching over each of us personally.

To recklessly abandon ourselves to the Spirit of God and experience His glory, we need to totally trust Him. He is everything He says He is for me alone, because He loves me.

If I were the only person who had ever lived on planet Earth, He would have come in the flesh and died for me. He is Comforter for me. He is Shepherd for me. He is El-Shaddai for me. His name is Jesus, and He has given me the right to use that name!

> **And whatsoever ye shall ask in my name, that will I do, that the Father may be glorified in the Son.**
>
> **If ye shall ask any thing in my name, I will do it.**
>
> **John 14:13,14**

Do you see that the Father is glorified when we receive from Him, using the Name of Jesus?

Open Doors in Russia

In 1993, God opened doors for me to travel in Russia for a month, ministering from church to church. Jim Kaseman Ministries arranged all the details for children's crusades, teacher training, preaching, transportation, and lodging.

Jim Kaseman is a special gift to the Body of Christ. Through his organization, Association of Faith Churches and Ministries (AFCM), he set up offices in Minsk, Belarus, and distributed 3.3 million books by Kenneth E. Hagin to the Russian people.

We probably will never be able to comprehend in this life the eternal implications of that one project. My trip alone constituted countless hours of planning and preparation on his part. I cannot adequately express my deep admiration for Jim and others like him who continue to labor in God's harvest field while others get the glory.

While I was in Russia, the Parliament Building in Moscow was bombed. Political upheaval set the mood for anxiety among the people. Citizens gathered around radios, not knowing what the next hour held for their country.

Tempers flared. Mothers stayed close to their babies. Each day the radio announced changes in the value of the ruble. The economy was in such a disastrous state of turmoil, the people needed to add imaginary zeros to the face value of their currency.

Peace Like a River

In the midst of all this turmoil, the church, with its many-faceted ministries, continued to operate in peace.

> **The Lord will give strength unto his people; the Lord will bless his people with peace.**
>
> **Psalm 29:11**

That peace flooded me like a river. Joining my faith together with Russian and American believers, it was easy to believe that God would see us through. We were the Body of Christ. Of what should we be afraid?

Based in Minsk, I traveled by train to Moscow, Vladimir, and certain villages. Churches would send drivers to take me to closer destinations. Once I was headed to Polozk. The driver, who only spoke Russian, arrived in an older Mercedes, accompanied by our interpreter and another young woman.

The interpreter explained our trip would take approximately two hours. Soon we were traveling an almost deserted road. The woods were dense and beautiful. After about an hour of seeing no buildings or gas stations, our interpreter asked me to pray that we might make it to our destination. It seems the ancient Mercedes was prone to breaking down, and it was low on fuel. I asked why they had not gotten fuel in Minsk, but she simply shrugged her shoulders as if she had no idea.

Traveling Through Bear Country

As I surveyed the surrounding woods, my mind drifted to a question asked earlier about bears. Yes, I was told, there were bears in these woods and, yes, they were the type that ate people!

It had been a long time since we saw any other vehicle, and that had been a horse-drawn wagon. As the sun began to hang low over the treetops, dusk caused an almost ominous appearance to the deep green woods.

Asking how much farther we had to travel, I was told it would be about half an hour. Would there be a gas station ahead? No, I was told; there was nothing ahead except more woods until we arrived at our destination.

Suddenly, our driver steered onto the edge of the road. The car came to a stop. The driver began to pump the gas pedal repeatedly. I kept asking what was wrong. It took awhile for anyone to answer me, as they kept talking excitedly back and forth in Russian. It seemed we were out of gas.

Empty and Going Nowhere

The driver hopped from the car, lifted the hood, and pulled out some part of the engine. Shaking it in despair, he related to the ladies and they told me, we were out of fuel. Whatever that part was, it was dry, which meant the engine was bone dry. Later, when I checked with a Mercedes-Benz dealer in the states, he told me the part was probably a fuel filter.

My knowledge of cars is limited to the make and color, so I am unable to tell you if the Mercedes was diesel or gasoline fueled. The U.S. dealer later told me that diesel models must have their fuel lines pumped out before they can be refueled once they have run dry. In any event, empty is empty, and going nowhere is going nowhere.

We were all sitting in the car, waiting. When I asked what we were going to do, the Russians got a bewildered look on their faces and did not answer. After awhile, our driver began to shout for joy. He saw a tractor coming in the distance. The interpreter sighed with relief and told me that everything would be okay now, because the tractor used the same kind of fuel as the car, and we would be able to get some fuel from the tractor driver.

Help Denied

Our driver ran down the road to meet the tractor. We were so happy. Half an hour seems much longer when you are sitting out in the middle of nowhere trying to start a car.

Then, to our dismay we saw the tractor driver refusing to stop, angrily waving our driver away while yelling "Nyet, nyet," which means "no" in Russian.

As the tractor lumbered past, our driver kept running alongside, begging for help. Finally he gave up when the tractor was well down the road. Then he walked to the car looking very dejected, jerked the door open, and threw himself into the front seat. Raising both arms, he poured out his frustration, which could be detected in any language.

It was then that the reality of the situation dawned on me. I could see myself becoming bear supper! There was a decision to be made. Was everything that "God is" simply for everyone else, or was it for me personally? This is the question each of us must decide.

I use the term "decide," because faith is an act of your will. You choose to believe God or not to believe Him.

Life in Jesus' Day

Can you imagine what it must have been like living in the time of Jesus? There was mass poverty, sickness, and disease. There was no penicillin or novocaine. Simple infections would turn to blood poisoning or gangrene. People were oppressed politically, physically, and spiritually.

As Jesus traveled from city to city, the crowds would press upon Him until the Scripture tells us He and His disciples had no time even to eat.

As we read the Gospel accounts, we can only try to imagine the sounds, smells, pushing, calling, and shouts of "Jesus is coming!" Was there anyone who had not heard? Jesus was making the lame to walk and the blind to see, and was raising the dead.

And they came to Jericho: and as he went out of Jericho with his disciples and a great number of people, blind Bartimaeus, the son of Timaeus, sat by the highway side begging.

And when he heard that it was Jesus of Nazareth, he began to cry out, and say, Jesus, thou son of David, have mercy on me.

And many charged him that he should hold his peace: but he cried the more a great deal, Thou son of David, have mercy on me.

And Jesus stood still, and commanded him to be called. And they call the blind man, saying unto him, Be of good comfort, rise; he calleth thee.

And he, casting away his garment, rose, and came to Jesus.

And Jesus answered and said unto him, What wilt thou that I should do unto thee? The blind man said unto him, Lord, that I might receive my sight.

And Jesus said unto him, Go thy way; thy faith hath made thee whole. And immediately he received his sight, and followed Jesus in the way.

Mark 10:46-52

Remember, Bartimaeus could not see Jesus. He had only heard about Him. Often, we cannot "see" how God can work out our situation; we have only "heard" that He can.

Bartimaeus' Decision

Bartimaeus made a decision. What he had heard others receiving was what he wanted to receive from Jesus. He did not just cry out, "Have mercy!" First he used the Name — the Name that is above all names. He was, in essence, calling, "Jesus, your Name is the Name that can save me." Then he went further, recognizing Him as the Messiah by calling Him the son of David.

Bartimaeus was actually entering into His presence through worship: "Jesus, thou son of David...." And now he puts forth his petition: "...have mercy on me."

In other words, Bartimaeus was saying, "I know You are Jesus to the crowds. I know You are the son of David to the crowds. I have heard. But now have mercy on me personally. Be Jesus for me. Be the son of David for me."

Notice Bartimaeus did not get into a long discourse, saying how long he had been begging by the roadside. He did not tell Jesus how hot it was sitting in the sun all day. He didn't go into any long stories about how he had to stumble helplessly to the Temple to make sacrifices. No, he just cried out, using the Name, claiming what he desired.

Attacks on Faith

People trying to shut him up made him cry all the louder. Have people ever tried to get you to shut up? Have they tried to convince you that you cannot have what you desire? Maybe they have told you healing is not for today, or that God is trying to teach you something through your sickness. Like Bartimaeus, ignore their hell-inspired admonitions. Cry out to Jesus for your answer, and do not let anyone shut you up!

When Bartimaeus approached Jesus, he was already in faith, and he had thrown aside his beggar garments. Jesus obviously could see that Bartimaeus was blind, yet He asked him, "What wilt thou that I should do unto thee?"

Why do you think Jesus asked him this? The reason takes us back to John 14:13,14, which tells us that God the Father is glorified in the Son when you receive the things you ask in His Name. This means that Jesus was, in essence, asking Bartimaeus to join with Him in glorifying the Father: "You ask, I do, and God gets the glory."

Boldly Asking Activates Faith

Bartimaeus calls Him Lord and boldly asks exactly what he wants. He could have continued to sit by the road wishing Jesus would heal him and never received his answer. Speaking aloud our request activates our faith for the answer. Bartimaeus' desire was to receive. What do you desire to receive: prosperity, healing, or peace of mind? Speak it out.

Jesus told Bartimaeus, "...thy faith hath made thee whole." Jesus gave us all things 2,000 years ago, pouring out total redemption through His blood. Now it is up to us to take hold of what He has already provided for us through that perfect blood sacrifice.

After the resurrection, we find Jesus, with every drop of blood poured out for us, telling the apostles:

> **Behold my hands and my feet, that it is I myself: handle me, and see; for a spirit hath not flesh and bones, as ye see me have.**
>
> **Luke 24:39**

Did you see that? Jesus is not flesh, blood, and bones. The blood has been given for you. This brings us back to our original question: Do you believe this is for you?

Decide.

Is He Jesus for Me?

That is what I had to do that day in Russia. Yes, He is Jesus who can miraculously feed the crowds, but will He perform miracles for me?

Yes!

Faith rose strong in my heart. If Jesus will make crooked bones straight, remove tumors, and straighten teeth for me, why would He refuse to give me a little fuel in the woods?

"Okay, everyone, listen." The interpreter began to interpret. "How many of you have heard of Kenneth E. Hagin?" They said they had read his books. I told them I had read in one of his books that God had put gas in his car once to get him to the next town. Did they think that God loves Kenneth E. Hagin more than He loves us? Of course not. We were all in agreement. "Well, we can pray, and God will put fuel in our car to get us to the next town also." Their expressions spoke volumes. I have never seen unbelief manifested so clearly without words. The driver just stared at me. "Well, do you want to pray," I asked.

He turned sideways, tossed his right hand over the back of the seat, and pulled his right knee onto the seat, like he was settling in for a long wait. Then, using his left hand, he motioned to the starter, seeming to challenge me, "Go at it. Have a ball trying."

Supernatural Service Station!

Bowing my head, I prayed a simple prayer, reminding the Father that He did not love Kenneth E. Hagin more than He loves us, and telling Him our need. I thanked Him for filling our car with fuel in Jesus' Name.

"Okay, you can start the car now." The interpreter explained my instructions to the driver. Condescendingly, he put the key in the ignition once again. This time, he kept his eyes on me so he could see my expression when it did not start.

To his amazement, the car started on the first try without the slightest sound of sputter or trouble. It was as smooth as an advertisement on television depicting perfection. Effortlessly, we rode the next half hour without incident to Polozk.

And in that day ye shall ask me nothing. Verily, verily, I say unto you, Whatsoever ye shall ask the Father in my name, he will give it you.

Hitherto have ye asked nothing in my name: ask, and ye shall receive, that your joy may be full.

John 16:23,24

The rest of that trip was filled with joy to the fullest. I am not telling you that if God had not filled my car with gas, I would have been eaten by bears. Although the possibility was slim, a car might have come along that would have taken in four strangers. However, I consider this to be unlikely in Russia, where fear is such a large part of the people's daily lives.

In my opinion, the stage was set for a tragic scenario. Suppose the worst had happened. Not recognizing that Jesus could save the day, I simply accepted my fate and we began to walk into town. A big Russian bear came along and ate us all for dinner. People would have said it was God's will. They would have said we cannot figure out His mysterious ways.

Actually, it would be no more His will that I die in Russia than it would be for Jesus' blood to be tossed away as useless. Sounds sacrilegious, doesn't it? You know what sounds sacrilegious to me? It would be people saying I had died for the Gospel's sake. But I would not have died for the Gospel; I would have died for stupidity. The Gospel is good news, not bad news. I am more than a conqueror in Christ Jesus.

Do you realize that if I had not called on the Name of Jesus, God would have allowed me to get out and walk? He would not have filled the gas tank with fuel. He would never have locked me inside and driven the car by the power of the Spirit into Polozk.

Precious Weapons

Names are for the purpose of calling people. In grade school, the teacher calls your name to see if you are present in order to mark the roll book. If you do not answer, you are marked absent.

The good news is that God has never been marked absent! His 80-plus names have been recorded for our benefit and given to us to use. In Revelation 2:13, Christ's message to the angel of the church of Pergamos commends them for two things:

...thou holdest fast my name, and has not denied my faith....

When we spend eternity with the Lord, we will have no further use for the precious weapons we now possess. Tongues will cease (1 Corinthians 13:8). There will no longer be a devil to use our shield of faith against. There will be no one to bind or loose. There will be nothing to cast out. There will be no one to win to the Lord with our feet shod with the Gospel of peace.

His Unchanging Name

The battle will be over; the peace will be won. This old Earth will have melted with a fervent heat. There will be a new heaven and a new Earth. Do you know what will remain unchanged?

The Name of the Lord!

When Jesus comes back to Earth with us after the Rapture to destroy the Antichrist, He comes in victory. The Bible tells us His Name is called "...The Word of God..." (Revelation 19:13).

Verse 16 says, "And he hath on his vesture and on his thigh a name written, KING OF KINGS and LORD OF LORDS." Revelation 22 further records:

> **And there shall be no more curse: but the throne of God and of the Lamb shall be in it; and his servants shall serve him:**
>
> **And they shall see his face; and his name shall be in their foreheads.**
>
> **Revelation 22:3,4**

We will go through all eternity with that Name in our foreheads. What more can He say to us to convince us that we have every right to use that Name?

Be a part of bringing about His glory in the Earth. Use what He has given you. Speak His precious Name. Love the Name, share the Name, and do all you set your hand to in the Name.

> **And blessed be his glorious name for ever: and let the whole earth be filled with his glory; Amen, and Amen.**
>
> **Psalm 72:19**

[4]Lester Sumrall, *The Names of God*. South Bend, Indiana: LeSEA Publishing Company, Inc., 1992.

[5]James Strong, *New Strong's Exhaustive Concordance of the Bible,* Hebrew numbers 6268, 3118. Nashville, Tennessee: Thomas Nelson, Inc., Publishers, 1992.

[6]*The King James Version.*

[7]Norm Robertson, *The Supernatural Church*. Charlotte, North Carolina: NRM Publishers, 1993.

Chapter 7
Hot or Cold

Have you ever read the Bible as if it were true? That seems an odd thing to say, but sometimes we really do read it like it is a wonderful storybook. If you think you do not read it that way, test yourself. If you really believe you will get back a hundredfold if you give, you would give your entire paycheck in the Sunday offering. Often we say things with our mouths that have not found a home in our hearts.

Earlier, I shared the story of moving into a new house and not having the money to buy food, but God moved on my behalf. Let's back up to the day I moved into that house.

My friend Donna came strutting through the door, making fun of the fact that no stove or refrigerator came with the house. She had walked through a door that was left open while I carried boxes in from the car. In a corner of the kitchen, on the floor, was my cooler filled with ice.

The house was the nicest model Kendall Construction built, and it was in a beautiful new neighborhood, but the special FHA financing plan did not allow for a stove and refrigerator.

"Well, Miss Smarty Pants. It is awfully funny that God was big enough to get you this house that you say came from Him, yet He is not quite big enough to put a stove and refrigerator in it," Donna taunted.

My faith was running high at that moment. The smell of the fresh paint was filling my nostrils. Everything was fresh and new. God had given me this house in spite of seemingly insurmountable odds. I was standing in the middle of faith manifested.

Donna had challenged me before on minor things. Once she asked me why having my own house was such a big thing to me. I explained that after six years of living with other people, how wonderful it would feel to be able to hang a picture anywhere I wanted. If I chose, I could even paint the whole house purple! Donna had challenged me that I wouldn't do anything like that; there were just certain things you could not do.

So there I stood with every square inch of the interior painted in soft lilac. Eventually, the house had royal purple carpet, and lilac flowered bedspreads, and so forth. If I lived there now, I would have to walk around with my eyes closed! At the time, Donna and I were both in our 20s. She had challenged, and I had accepted.

A Challenge to God

This challenge was different. This challenge had been to God. I felt like David must have felt when he heard Goliath challenging the children of Israel. David replied, "...for who is this uncircumcised Philistine, that he should defy the armies of the living God?" (1 Samuel 17:26). For the record, Donna is now saved and living for Jesus.

I looked up to heaven. "Okay, God. You heard what Donna just said. She does not believe this house came from You." I was talking out loud to my Father as if Donna were not even standing beside me. "Will You please give me a stove and refrigerator so she will know that this house came from You?"

The words no sooner left my lips when there was a knock at the front door. Upon opening the door, I was greeted by a beautiful black gentleman holding a clipboard. He said, "I have a refrigerator for you."

Do you know what I said? I told him I had not ordered a refrigerator, and there must be some mistake. He must have the wrong house. Patiently, he turned the clipboard around for me to read my name and address at the top of the invoice.

Paid in Full!

The truck was backed into my driveway, and as I saw my name on the invoice, I realized he had the right house. "But I have no way to pay for it," I said. He informed me that nothing was due; the order had been paid in full. I squealed in excitement, asking who had paid. He replied, "It's anonymous."

Throwing his clipboard into the air, I began to dance and scream thanks to God. Later, I found that the refrigerator had been a gift from a Bible study group I formerly attended. They had heard about my house not having a refrigerator and took a collection and blessed me anonymously.

"See, Donna. God did give me this house. This is proof. Look at my refrigerator!" Donna was now fuming mad. She asked if I thought she was an idiot. Did I think she would fall for that? She claimed that I knew all along that the refrigerator was coming, and I had set her up.

The delivery man was now rolling the refrigerator into place with his dolly. He was chuckling at the two of us arguing back and forth. My faith was exploding. I said, "Father, You heard Donna. She does not believe You gave me this house. She does not believe You gave me this refrigerator. Will You please give me a stove in such a way that she will not be able to doubt that it came from You."

Donna's husband had been driving by and saw her car at my house. He came through the front door, squeezing past the delivery man and his empty dolly, just in time to hear the end of my prayer.

"Does Someone Here Need a Stove?"

"Stove? Stove? Does someone here need a stove?" he asked. I told him my situation. He replied, "Oh, we have a stove you can have if you want it." Praise God, you'd better believe I wanted it. I turned to look at Donna. Her mouth was hanging open. Her husband asked her if she minded.

She said she didn't know where they had a stove. He reminded her that it came from some apartment they had rented. They had put it in their garage. Didn't she remember? It was under all the stuff in the corner of the garage. She remembered and agreed that he should give it to me. He then offered to go get it for me. He did just that.

Within about 45 minutes after I had prayed, there were a stove and a refrigerator in the previously empty spaces in my kitchen. They did not cost me a penny, and they were delivered to my door.

Donna's response? "Now I know you could not have had anything to do with that. It was my husband who gave you that stove." Yes, I did make her admit that the house, stove, and refrigerator came from God.

Miracles Within the Miracle

I have shared this miracle over and over throughout the years. Each time I tell the story, my faith is stirred, and I think about the wonderful miracle God did, supplying me with a stove and a refrigerator. It has only been recently that I have started to realize all the miracles within that miracle.

Do you realize that God had to have that Bible study group collect and pay money to a dealer at the exact moment they did to insure that the refrigerator would be delivered while Donna was sitting in my kitchen?

Situations had to be arranged in Donna's life to insure that she would decide to stop by my house when she did. Think of the planning it took to get Donna's husband to drive by my house while her car was there. Then he had to decide to stop.

He needed to walk through the front door precisely at the moment he did to step into the perfect plan of the Lord. All of this took place before I had even prayed!

God at Work

For years I had a very immature idea of God the Father. It was easy to picture Jesus. He would be walking by the Sea of Galilee calling His disciples, healing the sick, or praying in the Garden.

The Gospels filled my mind with all kinds of images. The Holy Spirit was sweeping into the Upper Room, charging the apostles with power, pushing Peter into the street to preach, and setting the world on fire.

Each time I tried to picture the Father, He was sitting on a throne. He wasn't up to much; He was just sitting.

What does God do all day? Does He sit, sit, sit, and sit some more? Is He lazy? Of course not. But what does He do all day? Let's look into the Word to find out a little about His day. We will call this "a typical day in the life of God." The Word says in Jeremiah 29:11 *(The Amplified Bible):*

For I know the thoughts and plans that I have for you, says the Lord, thoughts and plans for welfare and peace, and not for evil, to give you hope in your final outcome.

This Scripture shows us God is:

Thinking good thoughts about you.

Planning for your welfare and peace.

Giving you hope for your final outcome.

Second Chronicles 16:9 says:

For the eyes of the Lord run to and fro throughout the whole earth, to shew himself strong in the behalf of them whose heart is perfect toward him.

In John 14:10, Jesus says:

Believest thou not that I am in the Father, and the Father in me? the words that I speak unto you I speak not of myself: but the Father that dwelleth in me, he doeth the works.

This Scripture tells us He is the One who:

Speaks through Jesus.

Does the works through Jesus.

John 14:2 tells us Jesus is preparing a mansion in His Father's house for us, and the previous Scripture says the Father is dwelling in Jesus, doing the works, so the Father is:

Preparing a mansion for us.

No wonder eyes have not seen, nor has it entered into the heart of man the things He has prepared for us!

The Work of Creation

Now let's consider the preparation that is going into our future. We see God taking six days to create the world, then resting on the seventh. I must confess I had Him resting for the last 6,000 years. The creation week was a model of all of time.

> **But, beloved, be not ignorant of this one thing, that one day is with the Lord as a thousand years, and a thousand years as one day.**
>
> **2 Peter 3:8**

The same way the Lord was creating for six days and then rested on the seventh day, He has been working in the Earth for the last 6,000 years and is about to enter His thousand-year millennial rest with His people.[8] We are not far from the completion of 6,000 years. Imagine a mansion and dwelling place that God has been lovingly making ready for us for the last 6,000 years!

Prepared as a Bride

> **And I saw a new heaven and a new earth: for the first heaven and the first earth were passed away; and there was no more sea.**
>
> **And I John saw the holy city, new Jerusalem, coming down from God out of heaven, prepared as a bride adorned for her husband.**
>
> **Revelation 21:1,2**

A bride does not just show up at the church without preparation. She has spent months planning every detail. When I grew up, girls still had hope chests. I could hardly wait until I could turn 16, the age that I would be allowed to have one. Embroidery, lace, and all kinds of beautiful treasures were lovingly sewn or collected and stored along with young dreams for that special day.

When we see that holy city, New Jerusalem, come down, it will be a masterpiece to behold — lovingly prepared as a bride.

We see a prophecy of this in Isaiah 65:17,18:

For, behold, I create new heavens and a new earth: and the former shall not be remembered, nor come into mind.

But be ye glad and rejoice for ever in that which I create: for, behold, I create Jerusalem a rejoicing, and her people a joy.

Creation in the Present Tense

Notice the word "create" is in the present tense. Therefore, we see the Father is even now at work creating new heavens, Earth, and a holy city. Revelation 4:11 also puts creation in the present tense, using "are" as well as "were created."

Thou art worthy, O Lord, to receive glory and honour and power: for thou hast created all things, and for thy pleasure they are and were created.

Once you start looking for creation in the present tense, you will see it everywhere. It is like not noticing a certain model car until you buy one. Then you suddenly begin to see them everywhere.

And be renewed in the spirit of your mind;

And that ye put on the new man, which after God is created in righteousness and true holiness.

Ephesians 4:23,24

The new man is created, present tense. God is active creating "new creatures" all over the world. While we sleep here, it is day on the other side of the Earth, and people are coming to Him and being created anew.

Creating Hidden Things

In Isaiah 48:6,7, God explains He is creating the hidden things now. A reading of the 45th chapter of Isaiah reveals God making crooked places straight, breaking gates, cutting bars of iron, giving the treasures of darkness, calling, girding, forming the light, making peace, speaking righteousness, declaring things that are right, telling, and justifying.

Psalm 51:10 finds Him creating a clean heart and renewing a right spirit:

> **Create in me a clean heart, O God; and renew a right spirit within me.**

He creates the fruit of lips and heals, Isaiah 57:19 says:

> **I create the fruit of the lips; Peace, peace to him that is far off, and to him that is near, saith the Lord; and I will heal him.**

Philippians 2:13 shows our Father working in us:

> **For it is God which worketh in you both to will and to do of his good pleasure.**

Now let's quickly renew this cursory look into a typical day in the life of God. I use that as an expression only because life usually has a beginning and an ending; a starting place and a stopping place.

The Beginning and the End

The Lord, however, had no beginning Himself. He always was. He does not end. He always will be, and He is the Beginning and the End. So what is He doing? So far, we have seen that He is:

Thinking good thoughts about you.

Planning for your welfare and peace.

Giving you hope for your final outcome.

Running His eyes to and fro, looking to be strong for you.

Speaking through Jesus.

Doing the work of Jesus.

Preparing a mansion for you.

Preparing New Jerusalem as a bride.

Creating new heavens, a new Earth, all things, a new man, clean hearts, the fruit of lips.

Renewing a right spirit in us.

Making crooked places straight.

Healing us.

Working in us to will and to do His good pleasure.

God Shows His Love

This list is just a sampling of the many things God is doing. The main thing to note is that He is and that He became flesh, giving His life as His own Son for us. Now He continues creating, working, preparing, giving, renewing, and planning on our behalf. There can be no question of His great love toward us.

> **For the Lord God is a sun and shield: the Lord will give grace and glory; no good thing will he withhold from them that walk uprightly.**
>
> **Psalm 84:11**

As a born-again child of God, you have full right to every good thing. This Scripture even contains that promise. So why are refrigerators and stoves not manifesting when needed as an everyday occurrence? The reason has nothing to do with God's desire to bless us and, no, it is not that you do not walk uprightly enough.

Strong's Exhaustive Concordance of the Bible defines "uprightly" (number 8549) as "entire, integrity, truth: without blemish, complete, full, perfect."

Earlier, we established that you are a three-part being: spirit, soul, and body. We saw that the spirit has already been made perfect before God. The soul is the area where the Holy Spirit is always washing us with the Water of the Word to bring us to the complete whole man.

Walking Perfectly in the Spirit

What Psalm 84:11 is saying is for us to walk in the Spirit so God can bless us. Is that because over there, in the Spirit, is where we act perfectly? You do act differently when you are walking in the Spirit, but the key is that in the Spirit is where our "believer" works.

> **The spirit of man is the candle of the Lord, searching all the inward parts of the belly.**
>
> **Proverbs 20:27**

If you do not believe that God doing the miraculous is based on belief instead of perfect lives, just consider some of the great men and women of the past. There are many examples of internationally known ministers who had signs and wonders manifested in their meetings, yet they had severe personal problems. These ran the gamut from alcoholism to sexual vice. Some had sickness in their own body while God was using them to heal others. So why were they used so greatly?

The Only Requirement for Miracles

The only requirement for miracles is believing.

> **Therefore I say unto you, What things soever ye desire, when ye pray, believe that ye receive them, and ye shall have them.**
>
> **Mark 11:24**

These men and women believed God. They met the only requirement God places on the miraculous. If it is so simple, why aren't there more miracles manifested in the Church? Please note this carefully. I believe this is the key to releasing the glory of God in the Earth!

Years ago, I had a neighbor named George. The love and compassion of God poured through me to George. Older church members will identify when I say I had "a burden" for George.

People thought George was dealing drugs. He had a large, ocean-going motor boat, did not work, and kept a vicious pit bull dog at his front door. Each time I ran into George, I shared the Gospel with him and always offered to pray with him. George always had the same answer: "No, I'm too mean. I've lived too bad a life. My sins are too many." Nothing I said could convince him otherwise.

Salvation Can't Be Earned

We can see how ridiculous George's reasoning was. We need to accept salvation based on the blood of Jesus, not on our ability to please God. There is nothing we can do to earn the free gift of salvation.

> **For by grace are ye saved through faith; and that not of yourselves: it is the gift of God:**
>
> **Not of works, lest any man should boast.**
>
> **Ephesians 2:8,9**

Coming to the end of ourselves, we fall on the mercy of God, understanding there is nothing we can do to save ourselves. Then we are washed clean by the precious blood and become new creatures in Him.

If any person attempted to convince us we do not have the right to salvation, we would laugh at him. You see we, as the blood-bought, blood-washed Church, know that we know that we know the power of that blood that saved us.

Why, when we know that we are saved by grace alone, do we turn around and try to approach God based on our works or worthiness to receive our miracle? Do you need a miracle of healing? It has already been provided by the blood that poured from Jesus' back.[9]

Healing

> **Surely he hath borne our griefs** [literal Hebrew, sicknesses], **and carried our sorrows** [pains]: **yet we did esteem him stricken, smitten of God, and afflicted.**
>
> **But he was wounded for our transgressions, he was bruised for our iniquities: the chastisement of our peace was upon him; and with his stripes we are healed.**
>
> **Isaiah 53:4,5**

> **...and he... healed all that were sick:**
>
> **That it might be fulfilled which was spoken by Esaias** [Isaiah] **the prophet, saying, Himself took our infirmities, and bare our sicknesses.**
>
> **Matthew 8;16,17**

> **Who his own self bare our sins in his own body on the tree, that we, being dead to sins, should live unto righteousness: by whose stripes ye were healed.**
>
> **1 Peter 2:24**

That blood has already paid for every financial need you will ever have. Do you need a miracle of finances? Partake of the provision of the blood.

Prosperity

For ye know the grace of our Lord Jesus Christ, that, though he was rich, yet for your sakes he became poor, that ye through his poverty might be rich.

2 Corinthians 8:9

But thou shalt remember the Lord thy God: for it is he that giveth thee power to get wealth, that he may establish his covenant which he swear unto thy fathers, as it is this day.

Deuteronomy 8:18

If you read the entire eighth chapter of Deuteronomy, you will see that the emphasis is on "remembering God." (See verses 2, 11, 14, 18, 19.)

God gives you the power to get wealth, but it is in "remembering Him" that He is able to establish that covenant by giving you the wealth.

The last verse of chapter 8 says:

As the nations which the Lord destroyeth before your face, so shall ye perish; because ye would not be obedient unto the voice of the Lord your God.

Deuteronomy 8:20

Why would they perish? For not obeying the voice of the Lord. What was the voice of the Lord saying repeatedly in that chapter? "Remember God, remember God, remember God!" Deuteronomy 8 follows:

All the commandments which I command thee this day shall ye observe to do, that ye may live, and multiply, and go in and possess the land which the Lord swear unto your fathers.

And *thou shalt remember* all the way which the Lord thy God led thee these forty years in the wilderness, to humble thee, and to prove thee, to know what was in thine heart, whether thou wouldest keep his commandments, or no.

And he humbled thee, and suffered thee to hunger, and fed thee with manna, which thou knewest not, neither did thy fathers know; that he might make thee know that man doth not live by bread alone, but by every word that proceedeth out of the mouth of the Lord doth man live.

Thy raiment waxed not old upon thee, neither did thy foot swell, these forty years.

Thou shalt also consider in thine heart, that, as a man chasteneth his son, so the Lord thy God chasteneth thee.

Therefore thou shalt keep the commandments of the Lord thy God, to walk in his ways, and to fear him.

For the Lord thy God bringeth thee into a good land, a land of brooks of water, of fountains and depths that spring out of valleys and hills;

A land of wheat, and barley, and vines, and fig trees, and pomegranates; a land of oil olive, and honey;

A land wherein thou shalt eat bread without scarceness, thou shalt not lack any thing in it; a land whose stones are iron, and out of whose hills thou mayest dig brass.

When thou hast eaten and art full, then thou shalt bless the Lord thy God for the good land which he hath given thee.

Beware that thou *forget not the Lord thy God,* in not keeping his commandments, and his judgments, and his statutes, which I command thee this day:

Lest when thou hast eaten and art full, and hast built goodly houses, and dwelt therein;

And when thy herds and thy flocks multiply, and when thy silver and gold is multiplied, and all that thou hast is multiplied;

Then thine heart be lifted up, and *thou forget the Lord thy God,* which brought thee forth out of the land of Egypt, from the house of bondage;

Who led thee through that great and terrible wilderness, wherein were fiery serpents, and scorpions, and drought, where there was no water; who brought thee forth water out of the rock of flint;

Who fed thee in the wilderness with manna, which thy fathers knew not, that he might humble thee, and that he might prove thee, to do thee good at thy latter end;

And thou say in thine heart, My power and the might of mine hand hath gotten me this wealth.

But *thou shalt remember the Lord thy God:* for it is he that giveth thee power to get wealth, that he may establish his covenant which he swear unto thy fathers, as it is this day.

And it shall be, *if thou do at all forget the Lord thy God,* and walk after other gods, and serve them, and worship them, I testify against you this day that ye shall surely perish.

As the nations which the Lord destroyeth before your face, so shall ye perish; because ye would not be obedient unto the voice of the Lord your God.

Deuteronomy 8:1-20

God wants to prosper us. God desires that we have great wealth. Many books have been written by respected men of God expounding the multitudes of Scriptures that prove this, and some are listed at the end of this chapter for your further study.

The freedom contained in every Scripture is in remembering that God is the power backing those Scriptures. How do we remember Him? An example would be a person being so thankful for what God has given him that he says, "Lord, I am going to give You back what belongs to You from what came from You anyway."

The Law of Sowing and Reaping

The person begins to tithe and give offerings. Now he has entered into covenant with God in the area of his finances, and the spiritual law of sowing and reaping takes hold to bless him.

Give, and it shall be given unto you; good measure, pressed down, and shaken together, and running over, shall men give into your bosom. For with the same measure that ye mete withal it shall be measured to you again.

Luke 6:38

Yes, he is sowing. Yes, he is reaping. But the key is that the person has remembered God and chosen to obey Him. That is loving God. That was the first thing He asked of Adam: obedience. Loving Him is the first of the Ten Commandments.

Then one of them, which was a lawyer, asked him a question, tempting him, and saying,

Master, which is the great commandment in the law?

Jesus said unto him, Thou shalt love the Lord thy God with all thy heart, and with all thy soul, and with all thy mind.

This is the first and great commandment.

Matthew 22:35-38

Recently, I was in a meeting where approximately 13,000 believers had come together to worship the Lord. The speaker for the evening said several things I felt were a misunderstanding of Scripture, yet in that meeting I had the greatest experience of my life with the Lord.

The Smell of Harvest

About two-thirds into the evening, I, along with about a hundred others in the room, stood to my feet. The presence of the Lord was so strong, I needed to stand. The King of Kings had entered! Suddenly, the smell of rain filled my nostrils.

It was cold and mixed with the odor of fresh-mown grass. Later the Lord showed me that this was the smell of harvest. It grew stronger and stronger, and finally I heard the roar of rain coming. Then it started to pour. I was being drenched from head to toe!

I opened my eyes to see the rain, but it could not be seen with physical eyes, though it was more real than any downpour I've ever stood in. This wonderful experience of the latter rain being poured out continued for about 20 minutes. The speaker began to ask, "Can you hear it? Not everyone is hearing it. It's raining, but not everyone has ears to hear."

How could such a mighty move of the Holy Spirit take place when there had been some error in interpretation of Scripture? The Lord showed me.

Overcoming Error

The speaker had remembered God. During the entire evening, He had been putting the audience in remembrance. From beginning to end, he had been lifting Him up, extolling His praises, and leading the people to fall completely on His mercy and grace in an attitude of worship, worship, and more worship.

It is God "that sitteth upon the circle of the earth" (Isaiah 40:22). He has "measured the waters in the hollow of his hand" (Isaiah 40:12). He is "high and lifted up" (Isaiah 6:1). Our access to Him is by the blood of Jesus (Ephesians 2:18). If you try to enter heaven by any other door, you are following a thief and a robber (John 10:7,8).

Speaking our miracle and approaching the Father on the basis of our good works is just as ridiculous as my neighbor George trying to measure his own worthiness for salvation. The bad news is that George's son was killed. Satan had a cult ready, Bible in hand, to tell George he could become good enough to turn to God through doing good works. So George began his long, arduous task of trying to become good enough.

He is probably still researching his genealogies and other such burdens the thieves and robbers placed on him. Yes, it is a sad story, but it is no sadder than a blood-bought Church trying to figure out a way to bring about what is already theirs. Miracles are yours already. You simply have to believe in the power of that blood.

> **...Prepare ye the way of the Lord, make straight in the desert a highway for our God.**
>
> **Every valley shall be exalted, and every mountain and hill shall be made low: and the crooked shall be made straight, and the rough places plain:**

And the glory of the Lord shall be revealed, and all flesh shall see it together: for the mouth of the Lord hath spoken it.

Isaiah 40:3-5

Prosperity Books

Kenneth Copeland, *The Laws of Prosperity.* Ft. Worth, Texas: Kenneth Copeland Publications, 1992.

Ibid., *Giving and Receiving.* Ft. Worth, Texas: Kenneth Copeland Publications, 1991.

Dr. Frederick K. C. Price, *Prosperity on God's Terms.* Tulsa, Oklahoma: Harrison House, Inc., 1990.

Ibid., *High Finance.* Tulsa, Oklahoma: Harrison House, Inc., 1984.

Charles Capps, *Seedtime and Harvest.* Tulsa, Oklahoma: Harrison House, Inc., 1988.

[8] Daniel's seventieth week will take place before the Millennium and after the Rapture. Charlotte Rahrig, *Faith-Guarding Kids In Troubled Times*. Tulsa, Oklahoma: Harrison House., Inc., 1996.

[9] Kenneth E. Hagin, *God's Medicine*. Tulsa, Oklahoma: Kenneth Hagin Ministries, 1992.

Part 3

The Glory of God Manifested Through Protection

Chapter 8
Wallpaper Mom

Our home was a very unusual place. Mom was a minister of the Gospel, and our home was dedicated to Jesus. Mom's ministry was of an uncommon sort. Any night you could find pimps, prostitutes, or drug dealers at our dining room table. They would come as strangers to our door at midnight or 2 a.m. and often leave as friends.

Over and over again, they would arrive in varying degrees of fallen humanity and then meet Jesus at that table. The draw? Mom never judged a single one. They came to her drunk, stoned, or dressed for the evening's work. Not once would she point out their sin. God placed no price on salvation other than to receive it.

Opening her Bible, Mom would share the Good News and allow the love of God to do its work. Over and over, new creatures left that table. There seemed to be some sort of underground network among the fallen, bruised, and broken passing our address from one to the other and always coming under the cover of night.

Drawbacks to Mom's Ministry

This ministry was not without its drawbacks. There were some close calls snatching these souls from the gates of hell. Bill was a young man who came from a very messed-up background. He loved Mom and wanted all she shared to be true. A judge had released Bill into Mom's custody as a last chance before sending him to prison after Mom had gone to court and pleaded on his behalf.

Now Bill wanted to live right, but he had only known one way of living all his life. As a small boy, he had been sent to the grocery store to steal groceries for the family's meals!

Bill continued his lifestyle, unknown to Mom, while he lived in the protection of our house. Stolen cars, drug deals, and Mafia dealings had long since replaced the stolen groceries.

One evening I came home from church to find the front door broken down. What a terrible feeling it is to see your front door half broken, hanging on its hinges, with gold plexiglass and wood bits strewn across the floor.

A Drug Deal Gone Bad

Mom and a friend were sitting inside, drinking tea and discussing the events of the evening. It seems Bill had completed a drug sale for $10,000 in Miami. When the man had handed Bill the money, somehow Bill had handcuffed the man to a telephone pole and escaped with the money and the drugs! Later, we were to discover that the money was hidden under my mattress. Bill was nowhere to be found.

Mom had been sitting at her table, and the man who had been handcuffed to the telephone pole broke our door down. He hadn't even bothered to knock; he had just exploded through the door. Then he had grabbed Mom by the neck of her blouse and thrown her up against the wall, furiously shouting while shoving a cocked shotgun in her stomach, "I want my money and Bill right now, or you're going to be wallpaper!"

Mom just started laughing at the absurdity of the situation. Try to picture this scene. Here is a woman in her 50s shoved against the wall by a very strong man. He is using his left hand to hold her against the wall, and in his right hand is a cocked shotgun pushed into her stomach. He is screaming demands, and she is laughing.

She asked him, "Don't you know who I am?"

Puzzled, he asked, "No, who?" Possibly he thought he had accidentally stumbled onto some high-ranking gangster's relative because of her confidence.

One Woman's Confidence

"Why, I'm a child of the living God! You can't hurt me. I belong to Jesus. In fact, you could pull that trigger and your gun would not fire."

Angrily, he pulled the trigger. The gun would not fire. His mouth dropped open while a look of disbelief covered his face. Mom gently took his wrist and led the dumbstruck thug to her table. Then she led him to the Lord.

He told her he had just murdered a man in Miami. She went with him to the police station, where he turned himself in. I don't know what became of him, because that was more than 30 years ago, but I know his eternal destiny. If he is not already there, he will be spending eternity with Jesus!

A New Creature

Bill turned up in a few days, squared everything with Mom, God, and the law, finding grace yet again. Unbelievably, the judge released him once again to Mom. This time, Bill truly changed. He became a real worshipper of the Lord and spent several hours each day in praise and worship.

When Mom went to be with the Lord, Bill took an emotional nosedive into depression. He has never yet recovered from losing the only person who was ever able to look past his rough exterior to the hurting little boy inside.

Although the last chapter is yet to be written in Bill's life, I know one person who intercedes daily for him in memory of a very special Mom.

Not Without Persecution

I wish I could tell you that Mom carried on her ministry with the loving support of her whole family, but this simply was not the case. She suffered much persecution and was greatly criticized and misunderstood.

My sister and I were very jealous of her time and were always resentful of "those people who are just using you." Dad worked nights at Pratt Whitney Aircraft, so he was spared most of the goings-on, but he still made occasional threats to have her committed. (Mom was not at the place yet in her Christian walk to understand submission and authority to her husband's desires, he being the head of the house.)

Family members were known to speak of her activities through curled lips, disgusted with the shame of the type of people she allowed in our home. No one thought of her as having a ministry. Even Mom didn't realize she had a powerful ministry. She just lived life the only way she knew how. She did not have it in her heart to live any other way. She stood alone.

Mom received no recognition from the church world either. In fact, I remember the day a member of the ministerial organization she was ordained through came to the house with a "witness" to remove her credentials. Mom, who had not yet learned of her covenant of healing, was in bed recovering from congestive heart failure.

Weak and hardly able to talk, she graciously listened to their charges and demand for her credentials. She asked me to bring her purse. Removing the card from her purse, she handed it to them without a word of objection. She simply told them she understood. Walking to the door, I was biting my tongue with fury.

Do Not Judge!

After they left, I ran into Mom's room crying, telling her how sorry I was and how terrible they had been. She simply said they did what they felt they had to do, and I wasn't to judge them.

This brings us to another key in seeing miraculous signs and wonders: Do not judge!

To Mom, no one ever did anything that was their fault. She was always excusing people. If someone gave her a certain finger sign in traffic, she said, "Bless their little hurting hearts. They probably just lost their job, or maybe their wife asked them for a divorce." If someone called her a name, she would remind me that hurting people say hurting things.

A famous movie star lived a few blocks from us before he landed his first movie. Mom had performed the ceremony for his wedding to my sister's friend, who was also a family friend. The marriage was a stormy one filled with arguments that eventually turned violent.

Once when he had beaten his wife up, she called the police, and he ran to our house to hide. His wife knew that was where he would go. The police came, and Mom asked them to give her time to talk to him. She did, and they walked out together to the police car.

After the police took him away, I let Mom know that I thought he was about the lowest skunk I had ever seen. Wife-beaters should be locked up and the key thrown away, I added. Mom just said, "Cookie, you should be thanking God that you have not had to live his life. You might not have done so well."

Protecting the Anointing

I just could not understand her. She wouldn't say a derogatory word against a wife-beater! Now I understand. She was guarding the anointing.

For he shall have judgment without mercy, that hath shewed no mercy; and mercy rejoiceth against judgment.

James 2:13

The key phrase in that Scripture is "mercy rejoiceth against judgment." At different times, I have tried to not judge people. This is a very difficult task to attempt in your own strength. Satan made certain to bring unlovable people across my path to thwart my efforts. It was like trying to hold back an ocean wave with your hand. There was just no way.

God never meant for us to try to keep the royal law of love in our own strength. It takes the power of His Holy

Spirit. His mercy flowing through us will rejoice at the opportunity to not judge.

A Need for Mercy

When Jesus sent messengers ahead of Him into a village of the Samaritans to make ready for His visit, they refused Him. The disciples became very angry and said:

> **...Lord, wilt thou that we command fire to come down from heaven, and consume them, even as Elias did?**
>
> **Luke 9:54**

They were operating in their own strength, their own patience, and their own measure of justice. Beside them stood mercy indwelling Jesus, the One who had told them it would be better for Him to leave so the Comforter could come. They needed that mercy to indwell them and flow through them to the world.

> **But he turned, and rebuked them, and said, Ye know not what manner of spirit ye are of.**
>
> **For the Son of man is not come to destroy men's lives, but to save them. And they went to another village.**
>
> **Luke 9:55,56**

Judgment Destroys Lives!

The disciples wanted judgment. Jesus gave mercy instead and told them He did not come to destroy men's lives. Did you catch that? *Judgment destroys lives!* Jesus carried this mercy all the way to the cross, asking the Father to forgive those who had crucified Him, for they did not know what they were doing.

As we saw in the last chapter, the only requirement for miracles is believing. It is true. There is absolutely no other requirement. You might ask, "Why say that it is important to not judge if you want to walk in the miraculous?"

Think for a moment about the last time you were judging someone. Were you angry over something they had done? Or someone they had hurt? Maybe it was a situation where you were angry over those who bombed the Federal Building in Oklahoma City, killing innocent little children.

Think about how you felt at the moment you were in judgment. Now try to think about believing God for something at that moment. Not only will you be unable to believe God at that moment, but you will not want to.

Faith vs. Judgment

When we get angry and judge, it is over something that has happened. It is over something someone has done or is going to do. In other words, be it a year, a minute, or a second ago, it is not now. Faith, on the other hand, is "now." You cannot be in faith at the same moment you are in judgment.

> **Now faith is the substance of things hoped for, the evidence of things not seen.**
>
> **Hebrews 11:1**

The Bible has a great deal to say about the power of agreement. Usually we think about agreement in the areas of the promises of God and our authority.

> **Again I say unto you, that if two of you shall agree on earth as touching any thing that they shall ask, it shall be done for them of my Father which is in heaven.**
>
> **For where two or three are gathered together in my name, there am I in the midst of them.**
>
> **Matthew 18:19,20**

Notice that when the two are in agreement, Jesus is there in their midst to bring it to pass. He says in this Scripture that is the reason it will come to pass; agreement brings His presence into their midst.

Counterfeit Kingdom

The kingdom of Satan is a counterfeit of the kingdom of God. The devil is not a creator. He can only copy God in reverse! If you want to know how the kingdom of heaven works, just reverse what you see in the kingdom of darkness.

Giving instead of being stingy, loving instead of hating, and so forth.

If there were a typical Scripture in a satanic "Bible," it would read something like this: "Do not give, and it shall not be given unto you."

Did you know you can agree with hell? Isaiah 28 is a prophetic chapter that speaks of the promised Messiah. In verses 15 and 18 it speaks of those who agree with hell in falsehood and lies:

> **...We have made a covenant with death, and with hell are we in agreement...**
>
> **And your covenant with death shall be disannulled, and your agreement with hell shall not stand....**
>
> **Isaiah 28:15,18**

The same way Jesus is in our midst when we are agreeing together for the things of God, Satan shows up in our midst when we agree with hell about people. How do we know if we are agreeing with hell? The answer is simple: Are we judging? Jesus excuses people; Satan accuses.

In the Book of Revelation we find the fall of Satan recorded:

> **And the great dragon was cast out, that old serpent, called the Devil, and Satan, which deceiveth the whole world: he was cast out into the earth, and his angels were cast out with him.**
>
> **And I heard a loud voice saying in heaven, Now is come salvation, and strength, and the kingdom of our God, and the power of his Christ: for the accuser of our brethren is cast down, which accused them before our God day and night.**
>
> **Revelation 12:9,10**

Satanic Agreement

Genesis 11 records a satanic agreement in the building of the Tower of Babel. We find the Lord saying in verse 6:

> **...Behold, the people is one, and they have all one language; and this they begin to do: and now nothing will be restrained from them, which they have imagined to do.**

That was the satanic counterfeit "power of agreement" in manifestation.

On a more familiar level, watch what happens when a husband and wife "agree" that their child is stupid and rebellious. They begin to speak their agreement, and because they have agreed together, Satan will come into their midst and be certain to bring to pass what they have agreed upon.

Spiritual laws work in the negative as well as the positive. If sowing equals reaping in the positive, then not sowing reaps not reaping in the negative.

Today you will be faced with many opportunities to judge people. As a children's pastor, I have always been deeply grieved when I observe the way children are treated by parents in grocery stores and other places where our paths cross.

Ugly, evil words spill out of frustrated lips toward little innocents who sometimes do not even realize that they are doing anything wrong. I want to say, "You're planting a crop, and you're going to reap the whirlwind." Or I want to hit the parents with my Bible while quoting Matthew 25:40, "Inasmuch as ye have done it unto one of the least of these...ye have done it unto me."

But I must guard the anointing and make a choice. I can either side with the devil and come into agreement with him in condemning the parents in my heart, or I can side with Jesus and say, "Forgive them, Lord, for they do not know what they do."

Then I can begin to intercede in my prayer language for the parents to be born again. I can ask the Lord to put a laborer in their path to minister the Gospel to them in an effective way that they will be able to understand. If I am not in judgment in my heart, God may well make me the laborer.

The Second Greatest Commandment

The unbelieving Gentiles in Romans 2 are showing the law in their hearts by either accusing or excusing one another. That brings us to the second greatest commandment:

> **...Thou shalt love thy neighbour as thyself.**
>
> **Matthew 22:39**

Do not judge a single one!

I visited a friend recently, and one of the other guests was pointing a finger at him, jokingly accusing him of doing something wrong. He laughingly told her, "When you have one finger pointing at me, you have three pointing back at yourself." As I looked at her hand, I realized not only were there three fingers pointing back at herself, but there was one pointing up at God! As Jesus said, "...ye have done it unto me."

Chapter 9

A Counterfeit Kingdom

Satan is the counterfeiter. As we pointed out earlier, if you want to understand how the kingdom of heaven operates, just reverse what you see in the kingdom of darkness.

The majority of people out in the world are clawing to make it to the top to attain recognition, power, and prestige, yet in the kingdom of heaven, you must become a servant.

Once you have lined your heart up with the heart of God, and you are ready to wash your brothers' and sisters' feet; and once you have laid down your will and said, "Not my will, but thine be done," you find yourself exalted. Your gift will make room for you, even bringing you before kings.

Oh, this is a wonderful backwards kingdom — backwards from all we see around us. For example, when it no longer matters that it comes to you, you will find yourself with recognition, power, and prestige. This is because it is the heart of the Father to exalt you. As a loving Father, He desires to give you all good things.

> **Fear not, little flock; for it is your Father's good pleasure to give you the kingdom.**
>
> **Luke 12:32**

There are those who would say that recognition, power, and prestige are evil. After all, just look around you. Many corporations are perfect examples of the fruit of looking for these things. Those climbing the corporate ladder are known to backbite, belittle, discredit, and even murder their competition on the road to success. Isn't this proof enough of the evils of seeking these things? Not when you keep in mind that Satan cannot create anything. He can only counterfeit, so what is he counterfeiting?

Recognition

And hath raised us up together, and made us sit together in heavenly places in Christ Jesus.

Ephesians 2:6

Power

Now unto him that is able to do exceeding abundantly above all that we ask or think, according to the power that worketh in us.

Ephesians 3:20

Prestige

The eyes of your understanding being enlightened; that ye may know what is the hope of his calling, and what the riches of the glory of his inheritance in the saints.

Ephesians 1:18

When Jesus allowed the prince of darkness to crucify Him (John 10:17,18), the evil one was not content to simply have Him killed; he desired to mock Him. He had men put a royal robe on Him and slap Him, spit on Him, and taunt Him. "Prophesy — who slapped you?" they asked Him.

Crowning Him with thorns and hanging a sign over His head proclaiming "King of the Jews" were further manifestations of the devil's passion to mock God. Every evil thing in this Earth can be traced back to that single goal.

Satan has a plot to rob every Christian. He plans to make you so disgusted with those who seek recognition, power, and prestige that you will not seek those things yourself.

God not only says He desires these things for you; He has given direction in the Word on how they may be obtained. For each and every good thing God has planned for you, Satan has designed a counterfeit to make you think it is not God's will. Here are a few examples.

God's Gift	*Satan's Counterfeit*
Drunk in the Spirit	Drunk on wine
Dancing before the Lord	Dancing in nightclubs or even in church, seeking attention to yourself
Peaceful sleep	Sleeping pills
Casting our cares	Ignoring responsibilities

You could continue this list indefinitely. For every good thing God desires for His children, the devil will bring a perverted picture to mind to try to keep you from reaching out and enjoying God's gifts.

This principle works in all things. The enemy tries to mock God in every truth in the Word. Consider the fact that you were created by God in His image. Just as Satan stood before the Lord, sneering that Job only worshipped Him because of the many things God had given him, he is doing the same thing today.

I can just picture him saying, "Oh, so You want them to know they are your children? I'll show You! I'll not only convince them that You did not design them; I'll go one further. I'll have them say they came from a monkey!" That is the ultimate mockery, when mankind, the creation God desires to share His throne with, believes such a satanic lie. This belief is even found in the modern Church in the form of theistic evolution.

Smoking: A Type and Shadow

When you begin to look around with unveiled eyes, you see the devil's mockery everywhere. But when the enemy is exposed, he is robbed of the opportunity to rob you. One good example is smoking.

The Old Testament Temple was a type and a shadow of the new and living temple, our bodies housing the Spirit of

God. Repeatedly, that Old Testament Temple was filled with the glory of the Lord manifested as a cloud.

> **And it came to pass, when the priests were come out of the holy place, that the cloud filled the house of the Lord.**
>
> **So that the priests could not stand to minister because of the cloud: for the glory of the Lord had filled the house of the Lord.**
>
> **1 Kings 8:10,11**

Satan's Mockery

Don't you think it is strange that in the Old Testament, the Temple was filled with a cloud, and today people everywhere are filling their new living temples of the Holy Spirit — their bodies — with a cloud of smoke from tobacco? The tobacco that is burned is the fruit of the ground, the same type of unacceptable sacrifice Cain offered before the Lord.

The gases in cigarette smoke contain thousands of chemical substances, including carbon monoxide, which readily combines with hemoglobin, a substance in the blood that leads ultimately to heart disease.[10] Think about it: Tobacco smoke actually alters your blood!

> **For it is the life of all flesh; the blood of it is for the life thereof....**
>
> **Leviticus 17:14**

The Word says the life is in the blood. Who could have hatched such an attack on us? What made the first man who smoked look at a tobacco leaf and say, "I think I'll set fire to this leaf and suck the smoke into my lungs"? It had to be inspired of hell. But why? Mockery. Mocking what? The counterfeit of what? There must be a true for there to be a copy.

The devil designed cigarette smoke to be a mockery in our bodies of the smoke of the glory cloud that inhabited the Old Testament Temple and the glory that fills New Testament living temples.

> **...for ye are the temple of the living God; as God hath said, I will dwell in them, and walk in them; and I will be their God, and they shall be my people.**
>
> **2 Corinthians 6:16**

The truth is, we are the temple of the living God. He does dwell in us. He does walk in us. He is our God. We are His people.

Manifesting God's Glory

Several chapters ago, it almost appeared like I was condoning sin by trying to convince you of your perfection in Him. It is only in seeing who you are and who indwells you that you can come to see sin for the despicable thing it is. You are the vehicle God has chosen to manifest His glory in this Earth.

I felt the rain and smelled the odor of fresh-mown grass while experiencing the outpouring of God's Spirit manifested as the latter rain. Psalm 72 is a prophecy of the fulfillment of God's glory in this Earth.

> **He shall come down like rain upon the mown grass: as showers that water the earth...**
>
> **He shall redeem their soul from deceit and violence: and precious shall their blood be in his sight...**
>
> **Blessed be the Lord God, the God of Israel, who only doeth wondrous things.**
>
> **And blessed be his glorious name for ever: and let the whole earth be filled with his glory.**
>
> **Psalm 72:6,14,18,19**

The Truth Shall Make You Free

The fourteenth verse says God shall redeem our soul from deceit. The truth is what sets you free — the truth about God, the truth about you, and the truth about the deceiver. Knowing the truth is the main thing the devil has tried to keep from you.

> **...If ye continue in my word, then are ye my disciples indeed;**
>
> **And ye shall know the truth, and the truth shall make you free.**
>
> **John 8:31,32**

The greatest truth there is runs from Genesis to Revelation: *You are not your own.*

What? know ye not that your body is the temple of the Holy Ghost which is in you, which ye have of God, and ye are not your own?

1 Corinthians 6:19

You are bought with a price!

For ye are bought with a price: therefore glorify God in your body, and in your spirit, which are God's.

1 Corinthians 6:20

Isaiah's Prophecy

Did you know one of the main ways God gave us to glorify Him in both our spirit and body is through our lips? The Holy Spirit indwelling and speaking through us to bring about His will in this Earth was prophesied by Isaiah.

For with stammering lips and another tongue will he speak to his people.

To whom he said, This is the rest wherewith ye may cause the weary to rest; and this is the refreshing: yet they would not hear.

Isaiah 28:11,12

There are many things that separate us as Christians from the world. Get a group of believers and non-believers in one room for any occasion, be it a wedding or office party, and bring up the subjects of abortion, politics, euthanasia, or homosexuality, and you will see the room divided sharply. The lines will be drawn in the sand, so to speak. Christians hold one world view, and non-Christians hold an entirely different view.

Tongues: Hotly Debated

Take a different group of people, all Christians, and put them together in a room. There is one subject you can bring up that will bring a sharper division than the previous subjects that separated the Christians from the non-Christians.

Brother will turn against brother, and friendships have been known to end over the debate. There is no more hotly debated manifestation of the Holy Spirit than "tongues."

Have you ever wondered why this is so? Could it be that this is where the greatest deception has taken place, because tongues is the greatest tool God has given the Church to bring about His glory in the Earth?

The second chapter of John records that the first miracle of Jesus was turning water into wine:

> **This beginning of miracles did Jesus in Cana of Galilee, and manifested forth his glory; and his disciples believed on him.**
>
> **John 2:11**

Miracles Manifest the Glory

Miracles manifested His glory! What was the result? This is when His disciples believed on Him. How significant that He was changing water to wine.

If you take a watered-down, ineffective body of believers and fill them with that new wine, they will begin to manifest His work on the Earth. They will cast out devils, lay hands on the sick so they will recover, and the Word says they will speak with new tongues!

> **And these signs shall follow them that believe; In my name shall they cast out devils; they shall speak with new tongues;**
>
> **They shall take up serpents; and if they drink any deadly thing, it shall not hurt them; they shall lay hands on the sick, and they shall recover.**
>
> **Mark 16:17,18**

I was saved for many years before I ever had a manifestation of the miraculous in my life. All I was showing forth of His glory was that my eternal home was going to be heaven. But God desires that this Earth be filled with His glory. If we want supernatural results, we must use supernatural tools.

Preacher With a Problem

A preacher from the Bahamas once came to my house, opened his Bible, and slowly read me the entire fourteenth chapter of First Corinthians, placing special emphasis on verse 19, where it says, "I had rather speak five words with my understanding, that by my voice I might teach others also, than ten thousand words in an unknown tongue."

He completely ignored verse 18, where Paul said, "I thank my God, I speak with tongues more than ye all," or the first part of verse 19. He failed to emphasize that the verse he was talking about was, "Yet in the church,..." he was so stuck in "my understanding is unfruitful" (verse 14). There was just no convincing my guest that Paul was addressing a problem in the Corinthian church, not outlawing tongues. I asked this preacher if he was a believer. He replied that he was.

Then I took him to Mark 16:17,18 that says that believers would speak with new tongues. "What, as a believer, are you doing about that Scripture?" I asked him. He went right back to reading First Corinthians 14 to me.

This time, he gave even stronger emphasis to his favorite passages, as if I had not heard them the first time. I allowed him to read the entire chapter once more. When he was finished, I asked him again, "As a believer, what are you personally doing about Mark 16:17,18?" He said he had no answer.

I sent him back to the Bahamas with a copy of my book, *Faith Guarding Kids in Troubled Times,* and Kenneth E. Hagin's, *Why Tongues?* He agreed to read them, based on the fact that he could not answer what he was doing, as a believer, with Mark 16:17,18.

Tongues: A Supernatural Tool

In my first book, *Faith Guarding Kids in Troubled Times,* I shared the following story of the miraculous way God used His supernatural tool, tongues, on behalf of a man and his daughter. This subject is so vital to bring about the glory of God in this Earth that it bears repeating.

For more than a year, I was involved in hospital ministry twice a week. One time, the nurses asked me to take Gabrielle, my angel puppet, to cheer up a man who was in terrible condition. They explained that he had been in a head-on collision and his pregnant wife had been killed. His 6-year-old daughter, who had been in the back seat, survived. She was in the pediatrics ward. This man had so many bandages, casts, tubes, and traction aids, it was unbelievable.

The nurses said they had given him medication for pain, but each time one of them entered his room, he would begin to thrash in the bed and make grunting sounds, looking pleadingly, like he was trying to ask them something.

Silent Desperation

At first, they were concerned that the man was experiencing horrible pain, but they noticed that as soon as they left the room, his thrashing stopped. Due to his serious injuries, the man was unable to talk.

After hearing this background, I took the puppet into the room. Sure enough, as soon as he saw me, he began to thrash back and forth and make grunting noises. Walking up to him, I told him to be calm. Everything was going to be fine. I had come to pray for him.

Laying hands on him, I began to pray in my prayer language. I did not know where to begin to pray, because he was in such serious condition. Immediately, he grew still. Leaning over, I asked him if he was a Christian. "Blink once if you are," I directed. He blinked. "Are you Spirit filled? Blink twice." He did.

I explained to the man that the nurses were concerned, because they could not understand what he had been trying to say. Then I told him that the same Holy Spirit who lived in him also lived in me. The Holy Spirit would tell me what he was trying to say. I left him with that promise.

A Word of Knowledge

All the way back to church, I was praying in my prayer language for the man. It was about a 45-minute trip. When I was almost at the church, I suddenly knew what he was trying to say. Through my supernatural tool, "tongues," God was able to give me a word of knowledge about the situation.

Hurrying to the nearest phone booth, I called the nurses. "Have you told him yet that his wife and baby are dead, but his little girl survived?" They said they had not because of his weakened condition. They felt that he was not strong enough to take the news. They were certain his condition would worsen if they told him.

Boldly, I shared what I had promised their patient and how I had prayed. I explained that the Lord had shown me he was trying to find out about his wife. The torment of not knowing was doing him far more harm than knowing the truth. The nurses promised they would tell him immediately.

The next time I went into the hospital, the nurses met me with the news that I had been correct. As soon as they told the man the news, he never again thrashed in bed or grunted. The man eventually recovered, having fully depended upon God for the peace that he needed.

Help for a Traumatized Child

His little girl, however, had not spoken a word since the day of the accident a few weeks earlier. She was recovering physically, but no matter how hard anyone tried, they had been unable to get her to say a word. The nurses thought my angel puppet might stir her into responding.

She was a precious little black girl with the cutest little braids. As I entered the room, she glanced away and proceeded to ignore me, continuing to watch television while running her hands up and down the metal bars of her crib-like bed.

I was praying for the Father to give me wisdom as I endeavored to catch her attention with the puppet. She was not in the least interested.

Finally, I introduced myself, set the puppet aside, and told her I did not really like puppets that much, either. I told her I had really come to find someone to play a few games with me. All this time, I was crying out in my heart for help and did not cease to pray silently in my prayer language.

Playing Games

As she continued to ignore me, I started playing the shell game with three plastic medicine cups from her bedside table. Each time I told her to guess where the button was. When she didn't respond, I would pretend to be her and say, "I bet it is under three." I would act surprised when it was not and say, "Hmmm, how did she do that?" Then I would do it all over again.

Now she was watching. I never quit talking, first being myself; then playing her part. Eventually, when I asked, "Now which one do you think it is under?" she pointed to one of the plastic cups. She was wrong. I pretended I was her and said, "Now, how did that lady do that?"

I took the little girl's hands and said I would show her. Moving her hands, I showed her the trick to the shell game. As I moved the cup off the edge and let the button fall in her lap, I pretended I was perplexed, and asked, "Now how did that little girl do that?" She began to push the cups alone, and I made certain to pick the wrong cup each time.

This went on for about 30 minutes. Then I said I would rather work on a puzzle. Clearing the table, I began to work on a jigsaw puzzle, handing her pieces and then pointing to where the pieces should go. The entire time we sat there, I was warring in the Spirit and praying silently in my prayer language.

To her, I probably looked like a lady who was ready to sit there all day. The room became very quiet as she stared

The Revelation Comes

Then she spoke. "I killed my mother," she said. How could any person have known what was stirring around in that little girl's heart? Possibly she had been bouncing around before the accident and her mother had said something like, "Sit down before you cause us to wreck." A psychiatrist might have worked with her for months or years and still not have been able to find out what was troubling her.

On a conscious level, she might not even have known what the problem was. But the problem came to light using a supernatural tool, tongues. God has given us spiritual weapons like this that are unused and gathering dust most of the time.

"Your mother is not dead," I heard myself say, without knowing what was coming next. Praying in my prayer language had connected me to the spirit realm, so my response had been by the Spirit instead of by my mind.

I would have responded in the natural, "Oh, Honey, it's not your fault. Don't be sad." But the Holy Spirit responded with truth. Her mother was not dead. As a Christian, she had instantly gone to be with the Lord.

Hope Replaces Despair

I explained that we will all live forever somewhere and that her mother was with Jesus. Laying my coat aside, I used it as a demonstration of taking off this body. By the time I left that room, she had given her heart to Jesus and was talking like a chatterbox.

She was so happy that one day she would be reunited with her mother in heaven. She had been without hope, and hope deferred makes the heart sick (Proverbs 13:12). The Hebrew word for "deferred" means "prolonged." The truth brought faith, and faith brought hope "now," for faith is "now."

The nurses overheard the little girl talking away happily. As I left the room, they cleared a path around me, staring in awe, as if by some power of my own I had caused this child to be set free.

They saw me come in day after day, hanging little signs at the foot of each bed that said, "God loves you." Now they had seen God glorified.

Answers for a Hurting World

The Church has the answers for a hurting world. One of those answers is our supernatural prayer language that enables us to pray for the unknown and bring God's will about in the Earth.

> **For he that speaketh in an unknown tongue speaketh not unto men, but unto God: for no man understandeth him; howbeit in the spirit he speaketh mysteries.**
>
> **1 Corinthians 14:2**

> **Likewise the Spirit also helpeth our infirmities: for we know not what we should pray for as we ought: but the Spirit itself maketh intercession for us with groanings which cannot be uttered.**
>
> **And he that searcheth the hearts knoweth what is the mind of the Spirit, because he maketh intercession for the saints according to the will of God.**
>
> **Romans 8:26,27**

Time Will Be No More

If ever there was a time when the Church needed the mind of the Spirit, it is in these end times. The last seconds are ticking away. Soon, "time will be no more." One translation of that Scripture is that there will be no more delay. Whichever is correct, we know that the end of all things is at hand.

> **But the end of all things is at hand: be ye therefore sober, and watch unto prayer.**
>
> **1 Peter 4:7**

That word "watch" in the Greek means "to keep sober." Do not get so drunk on the cares and worries of this world that you become as drunkards stumbling through life, not knowing where you are going.

We are to be sharp, alert, and praying the mind of the Spirit. This leads me to the miracle this chapter was named after.

An Ominous Feeling

During a certain week, I was praying for the children in our church. A sense of urgency came over me, and I had an overwhelming feeling that a child was going to be stolen. Even after praying, I had no relief from the feeling that a child was about to be stolen.

I went to the pastor and explained what the Lord was showing me. He joined me in praying and told me to take whatever steps were necessary to insure the safety of the children.

This burden only increased over the next two weeks. I talked to each teacher, and we put additional security measures in place in each class. On Wednesday evenings we met in a hotel downtown. All the children would be with me and a helper or two in one large room.

The feeling of danger was so intense, one Wednesday I actually pulled my chair up against the door and sat there the whole service.

Each day, I continued to pray. Each day, the feeling got stronger. Not knowing the details, I used my prayer language to pray the mind of the Spirit. I was praying for the unknown.

The Stage Is Set

There was an 8-year-old boy in my class who came from a broken home. His mother attended our church and, at her request, one of our pastors worked with the boy's father and was instrumental in his becoming born again. The pastor then got the man plugged into another Spirit-filled congregation in our town.

The boy was spending the weekend with his father. A man the father had had drug dealings with before becoming born again came into the house and shot the father and his roommate, killing them both.

He then fired two shots point-blank at the boy. The boy said he felt the heat of the bullets as they detoured around either side of his body from point-blank range.

This is a direct quote from the local newspaper:

> Wellington — An eight-year-old boy witnessed the shotgun slaying of his father and another man in their home Sunday morning, and detectives believe the killer intended to shoot the boy, too.
>
> The child escaped unharmed, though, and called for help...
>
> "After looking at the crime scene, there is no doubt in my mind he was trying to shoot the little boy, too," Detective Sergeant Springer said.

Did you notice that the secular press did not mention how a grown man who has just killed two other grown men, armed with a shotgun, could "try to shoot" an 8-year-old boy and not be able to do it?

The Burden Lifts

The next morning, I opened the newspaper and saw an article about a child who was left behind in a playground by a day care center worker and was temporarily lost. It put me in remembrance of the burden I had been praying about for the previous two weeks. But when I started to pray again, to my surprise, the burden was gone.

No longer was there any urgency. No longer did I have a pressing feeling that a child was about to be stolen. I didn't understand. I hadn't connected the two incidents.

I sought the Lord. Had someone repented and decided not to steal a child? It puzzled me. Then the Lord showed me the child who was about to be "stolen" was the boy from my class. The devil was the one who was going to try to steal him. He was going to try to steal his very life!

Spiritual Weapons

But now not only will the boy live; he will be able to fulfill God's call on his life. No wonder the devil fights tongues so hard. No wonder so many are deceived into laying aside this great spiritual weapon that is such a vital part of our armor.

> **Finally, my brethren, be strong in the Lord, and in the power of his might.**
>
> **Put on the whole armour of God, that ye may be able to stand against the wiles of the devil.**
>
> **For we wrestle not against flesh and blood, but against principalities, against powers, against the rulers of the darkness of this world, against spiritual wickedness in high places.**
>
> **Wherefore take unto you the whole armour of God, that ye may be able to withstand in the evil day, and having done all, to stand.**
>
> **Stand therefore, having your loins girt about with truth, and having on the breastplate of righteousness;**
>
> **And your feet shod with the preparation of the gospel of peace;**
>
> **Above all, taking the shield of faith, wherewith ye shall be able to quench all the fiery darts of the wicked.**
>
> **And take the helmet of salvation, and the sword of the Spirit, which is the word of God:**
>
> ***Praying always with all prayer and supplication in the Spirit,* and watching thereunto with all perseverance and supplication for all saints.**
>
> **Ephesians 6:10-18**

According to this Scripture, if we are not praying in the Spirit, we are not fully equipped to stand against the wiles of the devil, and we will not be able to stand in the evil day.

I do not know how recently you have taken a good look around you, but this is the evil day! We must be strong in the power of His might. Every piece of armor is like a fully armed tank. Praying in the Spirit is the "gasoline" that empowers the tank to go in and take enemy territory, blowing apart the strongholds of the enemy.

An Unction To Pray

When my son Jacob was 6, we moved into a new home in Florida. Huge dump trucks would barrel down our street filled with sand being dredged from a canal at the end of the street.

One day I was washing dishes and praying in the Spirit. I did not know what I was praying about, although sometimes the Lord will reveal that to us. Suddenly, as fast as I could run, I ran to the front door, threw it open, and let out a blood-curdling scream just as Jacob was about to be run over by one of those trucks!

I don't know why I ran to the door so frantically; I just knew it was urgent. Jacob was chasing a ball into the street. My scream stopped him in his tracks. The truck actually brushed against him! Jacob would have been killed had the Spirit not sent me running to the door.

God desires to save us much heartache. He desires to intervene in the affairs of this life, but we must pray — not only for ourselves, but we must bear the infirmities of the weak. In the first verse of Romans 15 we are told to do that. Then, in verses 6 and 7, Paul says:

> **That ye may with one mind and one mouth glorify God, even the Father of our Lord Jesus Christ.**
>
> **Wherefore receive ye one another, as Christ also received us to the glory of God.**
>
> **Romans 15:6,7**

A Common Language of the Spirit

As we stated earlier, we give God glory in our body and spirit through the fruit of our lips. What is the "one mind" of this Scripture? What is the "one mouth"? Believers from every part of the Earth are joined together by one common language of the Spirit. What are we saying when we pray in this language? The one mind of the Spirit.

Joining together with one mind and mouth to glorify God is the only way we will ever become one, In this way, we lay down our lives for our brethren, taking time to pray for them.

> **I exhort therefore, that, first of all, supplications, prayers, intercessions, and giving of thanks, be made for all men.**
>
> **1 Timothy 2:1**

We become watchmen at the gates of our cities, praying God's will in the Earth so His glory can be manifested. Psalm 24:7 says, " Lift up your heads, O ye gates..." "Gates" here means in the Hebrew "to act as a gatekeeper at the city door." You are the gates. You have a head. A steel or wooden gate cannot lift up its head.

> **Lift up your heads, O ye gates: and be ye lift up, ye everlasting doors....**
>
> **Psalm 24:7**

"Doors" here in the Hebrew means "to loosen, open wide, and let go free." You are both the gate and the door. Open wide for the Lord. You are His entrance into your city!

> **...and the King of glory shall come in.**
>
> **Who is this King of glory? The Lord strong and mighty, the Lord mighty in battle.**
>
> **Lift up your heads, O ye gates; even lift them up, ye everlasting doors; and the King of glory shall come in.**
>
> **Who is this King of glory?** ***The Lord of hosts, he is the King of glory.***
>
> **Psalm 24:7-10**

[10] World Book, Volume S, "Smoking."

Part 4

The Glory of God Manifested Through Love

Chapter 10

Angel on My Shoulder

God is so good! That is not just an expression. Jesus told the rich young ruler in Matthew 19 that "...there is none good but one, that is God...."

When the Lord gave me instructions to write a book about the glory of God, I did not feel in any way capable of obeying. Objecting, I told Him I did not know anything about His glory! To define His glory to me would be as difficult as trying to define grace. It seemed overwhelming. How could God possibly expect me to write a book about something I had no understanding of myself?

The subject was massive and almost elusive. In my deepest thoughts, I even considered it to be rather spooky — the cloud rolling in the Temple and no one being able to stand.

Then, for a split second, I thought of the old Cecil B. DeMille movie, "The Ten Commandments." As a child, I was terrified when the plague, shown as a cloud, came rolling through the streets of Egypt, killing all the firstborn among the people and the animals.

Panic set in. "No, Lord, I can't do it. I do not know anything about your glory." The Lord gently asked me, "You know about my goodness, don't you?" I replied, "Oh yes, Lord, I know all about that. I could write a dozen books about your goodness. You have been so good to me."

Seeing God's Glory

Then the Lord took me to a passage of Scripture. Moses had asked to see God's glory. The Lord obliged by allowing him to see a portion of His glory by making His goodness pass before him.

And he said, I beseech thee, shew me thy glory.

And he said, I will make all my goodness pass before thee....

Exodus 33:18,19

I pray that as you have read this book, the goodness of the Lord has passed before you. He loves each of us personally. Each of us is special, valuable, precious, and important to Him. He designed us in His image. He wants to guide us and live with us eternally. He cares about even the little things we desire.

I grew up in a traditional church. I loved the catechism pictures of angels. They were either tall, slender women with wings watching over children crossing a bridge or fat little cupids flying about the manger scene. After I began reading the Bible many years later, I discovered how powerful angels really are; they are mighty flames of fire.

And of the angels he saith, Who maketh his angels spirits, and his ministers a flame of fire.

Hebrews 1:7

Bless the Lord, ye his angels, that excel in strength, that do his commandments, hearkening unto the voice of his word.

Psalm 103:20

An Emotional Attachment

Angels shut the mouths of the lions when Daniel was thrown into their den. The angel of the Lord opened prison doors for the apostles. Angels camp about us to deliver us. These are heavy-duty guys. In my head, I now had knowledge of what angels really look like; however, in my heart, I still had an emotional attachment to my childhood illusions about angels.

One day I happened to be shopping in a Christian bookstore. A special display caught my eye. There on a swivel rack were little golden cupids. They were called "Angel on My Shoulder." Oh, I wanted one!

However, just as I took a card from the display, I remembered the truth about angels. "Wait a minute," I thought. "Angels are not fat little cupids; they are big, strong beings. I can't buy that. It would be a bad testimony to the children in my class."

After looking around the store, I returned to the rack once again. I wanted one of those little angels so bad! I decided, "This is ridiculous! I refuse to buy one of them. God would not want me going around with a cupid-type angel pinned to my blouse." I walked away from the rack with my heart still reaching out for that little remembrance of tender childhood memories.

To anyone who might have observed me, I just looked like someone who picked up a trinket, changed her mind, and put it back. I had not said a word.

Gift From a Stranger

That night we had a guest speaker at our church. The meeting had been advertised in the newspaper, and many visitors came. As soon as the service ended, one of the visitors walked to me. She extended her hand, palm down, and I could tell she was handing me something.

Hesitatingly, with a questioning look, I held my open palm to her. What was she handing me? As she placed the little cupid pin in my hand — the very one I had longed for that afternoon — she said, "God told me to give this to you." Then she disappeared out the door without a word.

I sat in stunned silence, my hand still suspended in midair, holding the little angel pin. It was still on the card that bore the inscription, "Angel on My Shoulder."

"God told me to give this to you...God told me to give this to you." The stranger's words were ringing in my ears. God loves me! He cares that I wanted that little bauble. No one else knew I wanted to buy that pin except Him.

The Blessings of a Miracle

He said so much to me through that miracle. It was like He was saying, "Relax, Charlotte. Don't get legalistic on Me now. Enjoy yourself. I desire for you to be happy. I love you."

There is one of those little angel pins in my jewelry box right now. I can't tell you if it is the one the Lord sent me or not. I think my granddaughter took the original one somewhere along the way, and this is one I replaced it with.

I didn't put the pin in a glass case and admire it each day. Definitely not. That's why God could send me that little pin. He knew I wouldn't make an idol to worship. It was simply a way to show me that He loves me.

The message came through loud and clear. He is so good and worthy of our love! His goodness is a manifestation of His glory. He is a good God. He heals, blesses, restores, builds, comforts, and loves.

His goodness is what leads us to repentance, according to Romans 2:4. Let's go back to His goodness passing before Moses. Even though each Old Testament story was true back then, it has an additional significance for us today. That is called "a type and shadow." This particular incident was a type and shadow of how God's glory was manifested then and is manifested now.

> **And he said, I beseech thee, shew me thy glory.**
>
> **And he said, I will make all my goodness pass before thee, and I will proclaim the name of the Lord before thee: and will be gracious to whom I will be gracious, and will shew mercy on whom I will shew mercy.**
>
> **And he said, Thou canst not see my face: for there shall no man see me, and live.**

And the Lord said, Behold, there is a place by me, and thou shalt stand upon a rock:

And it shall come to pass, while my glory passeth by, that I will put thee in a clift of the rock, and will cover thee with my hand while I pass by:

And I will take away mine hand, and thou shalt see my back parts: but my face shall not be seen.

Exodus 33:18-23

God was saying to Moses and us, "Look, if I showed you my complete glory, it would be too much for you to bear. You could not see my face and live. But I will tell you what I will do for you: I have a place at my own right hand. I have a Rock. His name is Jesus. Stand in Him. I will let you have just a glimpse of my grace and mercy. But there is no way you could behold a straight look into my full glory."

The Glory of the Lord

And, lo, the angel of the Lord came upon them, and the glory of the Lord shone round about them: and they were sore afraid.

Luke 2:9

Just a reflection of God's glory shining in a field at night made the shepherds "sore afraid." The Greek of "sore" as used here means "exceedingly loud great fear." I can just hear the shepherds scream out. What an awesome sight that must have been! Paul tells us we are seeing that glory only as a reflection, and even that is changing us.

But we all, with open face beholding as in a glass the glory of the Lord, are changed into the same image from glory to glory, even as by the Spirit of the Lord.

2 Corinthians 3:18

After getting just a glimpse of God's glory on that mountain, we find Moses coming down with his face shining (Exodus 34:30). It terrified the children of Israel so much that Moses had to put a veil over his face.

When Jesus was transfigured on a mountain before Peter, James, and John, His clothing became shining and exceedingly white as snow, according to Mark 9:3. Mark says the disciples were "sore afraid."

The Glory of God Defined

In the introduction to this book, I made two statements. One was that the glory of God is His Church; second, that it is, specifically, His goodness manifested through His Church.

I shared with you how I have seen Him manifest that goodness through healings, prosperity, miracles, and His desire that we show the world His goodness and glory by loving them and not judging them and by praying for them. In this way, we are a reflection of Him in this Earth.

If this book ended here, we would have had a good study of the glory of God, but it would not be a complete study. The best is yet to come. Jesus told the disciples in the Gospel of John:

> **I have yet many things to say unto you, but ye cannot bear them now.**
>
> **Howbeit when he, the Spirit of truth, is come, he will guide you into all truth....**
>
> **John 16:12,13**

After His resurrection, Jesus sent the Comforter, the Spirit of Truth, to indwell us. The Holy Spirit then began to guide the New Testament writers into the truth they could not previously bear.

Partakers of His Glory

We find Peter, who did not even know what to say (Mark 9:6), after he got a glimpse of the glory on the Mount of Transfiguration, boldly declaring that we are partakers of that glory (1 Peter 5:1):

> **The elders which are among you I exhort, who am also an elder, and a witness of the sufferings of Christ, and also a partaker of the glory that shall be revealed.**

So we see that there is yet more glory to be revealed than has been revealed thus far, and we are going to partake of that glory. Praise God!

> **For I reckon that the sufferings of this present time are not worthy to be compared with the glory which shall be revealed in us.**
>
> **Romans 8:18**

Unlike Moses in the mountain, we will be able to see God's glory face to face!

> **And there shall be no more curse: but the throne of God and of the Lamb shall be in it; and his servants shall serve him:**
>
> **And they shall see his face; and his name shall be in their foreheads.**
>
> **And there shall be no night there; and they need no candle, neither light of the sun; for the Lord God giveth them light: and they shall reign for ever and ever.**
>
> **Revelation 22:3-5**

The light will be the glory of the Lord. Think about it! We will not only see it face to face, but we will dwell in that glory forever. What a blessed hope! Jesus told us all we could bear. "Bear" in the Greek means "endure" or "receive." He told us all we would be able to receive.

A Place for Us

> **In my Father's house are many mansions: if it were not so, I would have told you. I go to prepare a place for you.**
>
> **And if I go and prepare a place for you, I will come again, and receive you unto myself; that where I am, there ye may be also.**
>
> **John 14:2,3**

Now we see the Holy Spirit telling John on the Isle of Patmos in A.D. 90 more details about that place He is preparing.

> **And he carried me away in the spirit to a great and high mountain, and shewed me that great city, the holy Jerusalem, descending out of heaven from God.**

Having the glory of God: and her light was like unto a stone most precious, even like a jasper stone, clear as crystal.

Revelation 21:10,11

Our Eternal Home

Doesn't that sound wonderful? God loves us so much, He is at this very moment preparing our eternal home. This chapter gives us an even more glorious description.

And the building of the wall of it was of jasper: and the city was pure gold, like unto clear glass.

And the foundations of the wall of the city were garnished with all manner of precious stones. The first foundation was jasper; the second, sapphire; the third, a chalcedony; the fourth, an emerald;

The fifth, sardonyx; the sixth, sardius; the seventh, chrysolyte; the eighth, beryl; the ninth, a topaz; the tenth, a chrysoprasus; the eleventh, a jacinth; the twelfth, an amethyst.

And the twelve gates were twelve pearls: every several gate was of one pearl: and the street of the city was pure gold, as it were transparent glass.

And I saw no temple therein; for the Lord God Almighty and the Lamb are the temple of it.

And the city had no need of the sun, neither of the moon, to shine in it: for *the glory of God did lighten it, and the Lamb is the light thereof.*

Revelation 21:18-23

John has told us that there will be no need for the sun, because God's glory will be the light of the heavenly city. He will be the sun. Did you know we will be just like Him?

Then shall the righteous shine forth as the sun in the kingdom of their Father....

Matthew 13:43

Glorified With Him

And if children, then heirs; heirs of God, and joint-heirs with Christ; if so be that we suffer with him, *that we may be also glorified together.*

Romans 8:17

Who shall change our vile body, that it may be fashioned like unto his glorious body, according to the working whereby he is able even to subdue all things unto himself.

Philippians 3:21

When Christ, who is our life, shall appear, then shall ye also appear with him in glory.

Colossians 3:4

So now we have come to the end of this book on the glory of God — and, lo, we find that the end is instead the beginning!

To whom God would make known what is the riches of the glory of his mystery among the Gentiles; which is Christ in you, the hope of glory.

Colossians 1:27

To make Jesus the Lord of your life, pray this prayer:

Heavenly Father In Jesus name, I repent of my sins and open my heart for Jesus to come inside. Jesus, I give You my life. I believe you died on the cross for my sins and were raised from the dead. I confess you now as my Lord and Savior. My sins that were like scarlet, are now white as snow and You have removed them as far as the east is from the west. According to Your Word, I am now Your child.

Signed ________________________________Date__________

Romans 3:23; 6:23; 10:9,10; John 3:16; 1 John 1:9; Isaiah 1:18

To receive the Baptism of the Holy Spirit, pray this prayer:

Heavenly Father, You said that if I would ask for the Holy Spirit you would give Him to me. I am asking You now to fill me with Your precious Holy Spirit that I may be a more powerful witness of Jesus. Holy Spirit, I receive You. Now, according to the Word of God, I believe I receive and am now going to speak in my prayer language. (Open your mouth and move your tongue in faith.)

Acts 1:4-8; 2:1-4, 17, 18, 39; 11:16; Romans 8:26, 27; Ephesians 5:18-20; Jude 20

About the Author

Charlotte Rahrig is a graduate of Rhema Bible Training Center in Tulsa, Oklahoma, and is an ordained evangelist with the Association of Faith Churches and Ministries (AFCM). She has taught at South Florida Bible Training Center, has been a workshop leader at international conferences, and has held seminars and published books in both the United States and Russia.

She has ministered with a daily radio devotional and has appeared on "The 700 Club," on Trinity Broadcasting Network, and with Dr. James Kennedy. She has also been a guest on "Point of View," a national radio show hosted by Marlin Maddoux.

Charlotte has authored the best-selling book *Faith-Guarding Kids in Troubled Times* as well as *Words* and *The Gifts of the Holy Spirit* coloring books, various curricula, tracts, and ministry manuals.

Her pastor is Mark DeBehnke, and her home church is Believer's Victory Church in West Palm Beach, FLorida.

Her vision is to be instrumental in ushering in the end-time revival, and her motto is: *"Preach the Blood. Win Souls. Know God."*

For information, write:
Charlotte Rahrig Ministries, Inc.
P.O. Box 700565
Tulsa, OK 74170

Recommended Reading

The Glory of God, Kenneth E. Hagin. Tulsa: Kenneth Hagin Ministries, 1987

Unleashing the Power of Praying in the Spirit, Oral Roberts

Why Tongues, Kenneth E. Hagin. Tulsa: Kenneth Hagin Ministries.

Recommended Tape Sets

"The Glory of God in You," Kenneth Copeland

"Tongues: Their Scriptural Purpose," Kenneth E. Hagin

Other Books by Charlotte Rahrig

Faith Guarding Kids in Troubled Times

Holy Spirit Coloring Book

Words Coloring Book

For ministry in your church, contact:

Charlotte Rahrig Ministries, Inc.
P.O. Box 700565
Tulsa, OK 74170